Praises for
Be Bullish Zero to Three

"*Be Bullish Zero to Three* is the guidebook I wish every new graduate received with their diploma. As a three-time Chief People Officer across fast-growing tech companies, I've seen countless early-career professionals struggle—not for lack of talent, but for lack of context. Ed gives them just that: context, clarity, and a confident path forward.

This book is packed with real-world wisdom, actionable advice, and the kind of behind-the-scenes truth-telling that HR professionals rarely put on paper. From demystifying onboarding and feedback to managing imposter syndrome and reputation, Ed doesn't sugarcoat the transition from student to professional. He equips readers with the mindset and tools to not just survive, but thrive.

If you're in your first job—or leading someone who is—*Be Bullish Zero to Three* should be required reading."

—Anja Hamilton

Former Chief People Officer, *Nutanix, Poly* and *IDT*

"The first three years of your career set the foundation for everything that follows. In *Be Bullish Zero to Three*, reminds you to stay curious, embrace feedback, and welcome challenges—they are your greatest teachers. Be intentional with your goals, build authentic relationships, and lean into every opportunity. Growth happens when you're open, brave, and willing to learn. At the end of the day, you're in charge of your career and growth—you're the CEO of You, Inc."

—Julia Anas

Chief People Officer, *Qualtrics*

"Success in your career starts early—especially within the first three years. In *Be Bullish Zero to Three*, Ed delivers a clear and actionable roadmap for new professionals looking to build a strong foundation. His insights align perfectly with the three principles I share with every new grad I mentor:

- Stay curious and stay humble
- Go beyond the job—consistently exceed expectations
- Own your results through strong personal accountability

This isn't just theory—it's a practical, no-nonsense playbook that empowers you to take charge of your career from day zero."

—Joy Wolken
Chief People Officer, *Pangea*

"*Be Bullish Zero to Three* is a practical guide for anyone navigating their first three years in the professional world.

As a Chief People Officer, mentor, and mother, I have seen firsthand the challenges new graduates face. This book provides powerful and actionable insights on everything from mastering OKRs and seeking feedback to understanding compensation and building crucial relationships that will truly accelerate career growth and foster long-term success.

It's an honest, insider perspective that any early-career professional could use to thrive."

—Megan Hansen
Chief People Officer, *Ontra*

BE BULLISH

ZERO *to* THREE

BE BULLISH
ZERO *to* THREE

WHAT NO ONE TELLS YOU ABOUT
YOUR FIRST THREE YEARS AT WORK

Edward L. Avila

BE BULLISH
BOOKS

Cover Design by: Marwan C. Harb
Author Photo: Kate Zotova of Pacifica Studios
Foreword by: Steve Cadigan

ISBN: 979-8-9993796-1-0

First Edition, October 2025

10 9 8 7 6 5 4 3 2 1

QUANTITY PURCHASES:

Schools, companies, professional groups, clubs, and
other organizations may qualify for special terms,
when ordering quantities of this title.
For information, email author at edward@bebullish.co.

"You're not just starting a job—
you're building a reputation."

~ *Edward Avila, the author*

Dedication

Writing my debut book, *Be Bullish 101*, was challenging, but crafting this second book, *Be Bullish Zero to Three*, proved even more difficult. It fulfills a lifelong desire to help others, just as I was helped early in my career by those who left lasting footprints for me to follow.

I owe my deepest gratitude to my wife, Mylene, and my son, Nicolas, whose unwavering encouragement and support made this second book possible. Starting over with this second book was both tough and humbling, but your love, patience, and belief in me kept me going. I am profoundly grateful and incredibly lucky.

To the next generation of leaders setting out to make their mark after college: Stay curious and embrace continuous learning. Equip yourself with knowledge and be bullish in making confident decisions. Your journey will have challenges, but with determination and insight, you'll find success and achieve your professional and personal goals.

To my peers and colleagues in the HR profession, whose dedication shapes the future of work: May this book honor the exceptional work you do every day and inspire others to follow your exemplary lead. Cheers to your ongoing success and lasting impact.

Table Of Contents

Foreword

We're living through one of the most extraordinary shifts in the world of work that any of us have ever seen. The seismic disruptions we've experienced—technological advancements, the global pandemic, and the evolution of workplace expectations—have left many questioning the traditional career paths we once considered so reliable. It's within this context that I'm thrilled to introduce *Be Bullish: Zero to Three* by Edward Avila, a timely and invaluable guide for anyone navigating the early stages of their professional journey.

If there's one thing that has become abundantly clear to me in recent years as I've studied the world of work, it's this: the old rules no longer apply. Career paralysis is real—and it's at an all-time high. Today's graduates face a unique challenge: how to make sense of it all amid more choices and potential paths than ever before. The sheer volume of options, combined with the pressure to make the "right" choice, can feel overwhelming. That's why Edward's book couldn't have come at a better time.

Be Bullish: Zero to Three is not just a guide—it's a call to action. Edward's approach to the critical "Zero to Three" phase of a career is refreshingly practical and deeply insightful. He provides a framework that demystifies this complex period, offering clear strategies to help you build momentum and define a path that's uniquely yours. His advice is grounded in reality, informed by years of experience working with emerging professionals, and perfectly aligned with the challenges and opportunities of this moment.

One of the key insights I've gathered through working with leaders and professionals across the globe is the growing need to adopt a new mindset about work. The days of linear career paths and predictable advancement are behind us. Today, success requires adaptability, continuous learning, and a proactive approach to career development. In *Be Bullish: Zero to Three*, Edward amplifies this message, encouraging you to embrace a mindset that's confident, optimistic—and above all—bullish about your future. It's about taking control, making informed decisions, and navigating your early career with the kind of boldness that sets the foundation for long-term success.

Edward understands that the first three years of your career are more than a stepping stone—they're a crucible in which your professional identity is forged. How you approach this period can shape not only your career trajectory but your personal growth as well. His emphasis on feedback, relationship-building, and continuous improvement resonates deeply with the ethos of *Workquake*. In a world where change is the only constant, these principles are your compass.

But perhaps the most powerful message in *Be Bullish: Zero to Three* is the reminder that your career is a journey, not a race. The pressure to have it all figured out from day one is immense—but it's also misguided. Edward reminds us that these early years are not about perfection—they're about exploration, experimentation, and growth. By adopting a bullish mindset, you're not just preparing for success—you're preparing to thrive in a world full of possibilities and ever-evolving challenges.

At a time when so many feel lost or uncertain about their professional futures, *Be Bullish: Zero to Three* offers clarity, direction, and hope. It's a guidebook for the modern professional—a resource that will help you move through the early-career landscape with confidence and purpose.

So as you begin this journey, remember: the future belongs to those who take risks, learn from every experience, and remain relentlessly optimistic about what lies ahead. *Be Bullish: Zero to Three* is your companion on this path—a mentor in book form to help you not just survive, but thrive in today's ever-changing world of work.

Welcome to the beginning of your career. Be bold, be bullish, and take charge of your future.

—Steve Cadigan

Talent Strategist, Author of *Workquake*, and Founding CHRO at LinkedIn

About Steve Cadigan

 Steve Cadigan is a globally recognized talent strategist and company culture expert with over 30 years of experience leading HR at some of the world's most innovative organizations. He is best known for scaling *LinkedIn* from 400 to 4,000 employees in just three and a half years and for shaping its legendary company culture during a period of hypergrowth and through its successful IPO.

Steve's deep expertise spans five industries, three countries, and dozens of acquisition integrations worldwide. His work has earned recognition from *The Wall Street Journal* and *Fortune* magazine for building world-class teams and talent strategies that thrive under disruption.

Today, as the founder of his own advisory firm, Steve helps leaders and organizations rethink how they attract, grow, and retain talent. Through keynotes, workshops and his podcast *Workquake Weekly*, he shows companies how to turn culture into a competitive edge—and empowers individuals to own their careers in uncertain times.

In a world where the workforce is more disengaged and change is constant; Steve offers practical optimism. He believes the future of work is full of potential—for those willing to adopt a mindset focused on growth, adaptability, and shared responsibility.

Message From the Author

If you've read *Be Bullish 101*, then you already know what I'm about—clarity, preparation, and taking your career seriously from day one. That first book was written for students and recent graduates trying to figure out how to show up with confidence and intention in a professional world that rarely hands you a playbook.

This next book, *Be Bullish: Zero to Three*, is about what happens next.

Your first job out of college can feel like stepping onto a new campus as a freshman all over again—unfamiliar, overwhelming, and filled with people who seem like they already know where everything is. But just like college, you'll eventually find your footing. The question is: how quickly can you adapt, grow, and stand out?

That's where this book comes in.

Be Bullish: Zero to Three is a concept that captures your progression from new graduate to early-career professional, typically over your first three years in the workforce. These years are foundational. It's when reputations are formed, your skills are tested, and your future trajectory starts to take shape. Unfortunately, many people stumble during this phase—not because they lack talent, but because no one ever explains what really happens once you're on the inside.

I've seen too many new grads and early-career professionals hesitate to speak up, get overwhelmed by unclear onboarding, or quietly struggle until they burn out or quit. That's avoidable—with the right insight.

According to a survey, 94% of early career professionals are likely to make a career move within three years of employment because their companies aren't giving them compelling reasons to stay.[1] That's a signal—and a warning. If companies don't give you reasons to stay, you'll start looking elsewhere.

I've written this book as your early-career accelerator. It's built around the **Employee Lifecycle** and offers practical advice across each stage—getting hired, onboarding, performing, being recognized, and ultimately deciding whether to stay or explore new opportunities. You'll get the same insights I've shared over decades leading HR and People teams at high-tech companies, helping thousands of employees grow from their very first day.

Along the way, I'll share real stories, useful tools, and behind-the-scenes lessons I've learned designing onboarding programs, talent development frameworks, and engagement strategies—many of which helped the companies I worked with earn recognition on *Inc. Magazine's Best Workplaces* list.

Let's not sugarcoat it: early-career professionals leave jobs quickly when they don't feel like they're learning, growing, or being valued. I've seen it happen too many times—great talent walks out the door simply because no one gave them a reason to stay.

That's why I wrote this book. To give you the inside track. To help you avoid unnecessary missteps. And to make sure you start your career path on the right foot—with eyes open, questions ready, and a bullish mindset.

Are you ready? Let's be bullish together.

—Edward Avila

Introduction

Experiencing something new, like a relationship, a vacation, a home, or a car, can be thrilling. This excitement can boost your adrenaline and make your heart race. With the right attitude and an open heart, each new experience can bring a version of that thrill. Every time you feel this unique excitement, you grow and evolve, seeing the world through fresh eyes and a different perspective.

One of the most crucial aspects of trying new things is approaching them with an open mind, heart, curiosity, and a sense of wonder. Exploring new ideas, places, and experiences opens worlds you never knew existed. You absorb these new worlds through your thoughts, senses, and emotions, gaining new insights, perspectives, and knowledge. Some experiences will profoundly impact you in ways you eventually realize later. Ultimately, this new understanding transforms the familiar and takes you out of your comfort zone, helping you grow personally and professionally.

Think back to the last time you felt such excitement—perhaps when you walked across the stage to receive your college diploma or accepted your first job offer. Remember how exciting and intriguing that was. But what happens when the excitement fades, and anxiety or stress sets in?

As you prepare to leave the university, which has been your home for the last four years, you may start questioning your future. *Am I ready for the professional world? Will I earn enough to cover my living expenses? Should I move back home or find my own place?* With high levels of competition, unemployment, and student debt, securing a job offer right after graduation can be a tremendous sigh of relief.

Earning money is often a significant motivator for new graduates when accepting a job offer, overshadowing professional development, career advancement, or company culture. According to a recent survey, 46% of college students say they'll try to make as much money as possible due to concerns about debt rather than pursuing their passions.[2] Many don't think beyond their first day of work or the details of the upcoming onboarding process.

According to another survey, two-thirds of college students struggle with the transition to the workforce. As a college student, you followed a daily routine and a structured course schedule with the guidance of an advisor. In contrast, starting a new job can bring a high level of uncertainty and can be intimidating as you enter adulthood with greater freedom than you experienced in college.

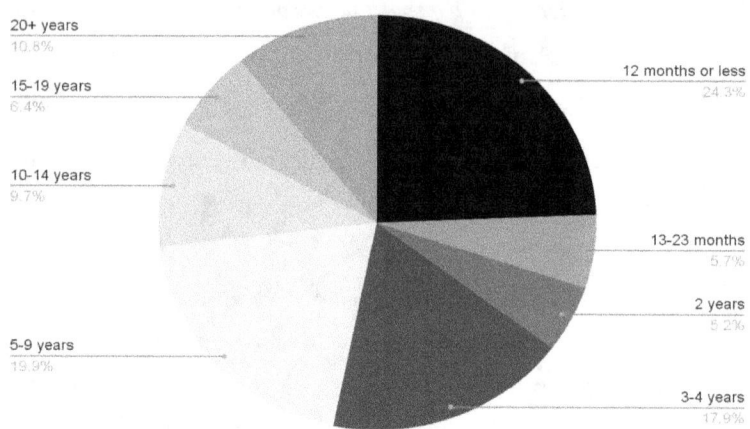

Table 0.1: Distribution of Employee Tenure in the US

Research shows that various factors influence the average employee tenure with a company. Approximately 35% of the workforce stays with their company for less than two years, and within this number, 24.3% leave within the first 12 months (see **Table 0.1).**[3]

This data highlights the challenges new employees face in adjusting to their new roles and environments. The same research shows that the median employee tenure for those aged 20-24 years is 1.3 years for men and 1.1 years for women (see **Table 0.2**).[4] Understanding these statistics underscores the importance of proactive preparation and continuous learning as you navigate the early stages of your career.

Age	Average	Men	Women
16-17	0.7	0.7	0.6
18-19	0.7	0.7	0.8
20-24	1.2	1.3	1.1
25-34	2.8	2.9	2.7
35-44	4.7	5.0	4.5
45-54	6.9	7.5	6.3
55-64	9.8	10.0	9.5
65+	9.9	9.7	10.0

Table 0.2: Median Years of Employee Tenure by Age

Another report by the US Bureau of Labor Statistics shows that 55.3% of recent college graduates leave their first job within the first year after graduation. This high attrition rate poses a significant challenge for new graduates, as leaving prematurely can hinder their ability to acquire the essential skills and experience needed to be competitive in the job market and to build rewarding careers. Staying in their initial roles longer with meaningful guidance helps them build a strong foundation, gain "hands-on" experience, and enhance their value to potential employers. **This is a BIG issue.**

Introducing the *"Zero to Three"* concept—the first three years of your professional career after graduation. This critical period can shape your future trajectory and is filled with both opportunities and challenges. The professional world can be both exciting and overwhelming.

As the data shows, recent graduates often feel more inclined to leave a job if they quickly sense it's not the right fit or if the work lacks personal meaning. Data shows that if they don't connect with the role, the team, or the organization, they are likely to seek a new opportunity rather than try to resolve their dissatisfaction. *Why should they stay if they are unhappy?*

While interviewing for your first job, many college graduates may not know exactly what they want or what to look for in an employer. As a result, they might not ask the right questions, and that's okay. This skill will develop over time as you continue your professional journey.

To succeed and start your career on the right foot, you must adapt to new responsibilities, build new relationships, and assimilate into a work culture that is different from college life. Adjusting to your first job can feel like a difficult process, especially after spending three to four years—or more—in college. Although initially daunting, this uncharted territory offers immense growth and opportunities to expand your knowledge and strengthen your skills.

However, don't leave your experience to chance. There are many unknowns, such as: *What should you do? Who should you ask for help? Where should you spend your time? Are you doing this right?*

Over the last three decades, I have worked as a Talent Acquisition Executive and led Human Resources teams in both startup and corporate environments. During this time, I have seen many college graduates join companies and, regrettably, conducted many exit interviews with them as well. The data gathered from these exit interviews provided me valuable insights into the factors influencing their decision to leave the organization. Those who chose to leave with less than one year of service commonly cited the following reasons:

- Dissatisfied with colleagues
- Lack of feedback from the manager
- Lack of career development or career advancement
- Lack of day-to-day support
- Support for professional development
- Dissatisfied with the nature of the work
- Insufficient onboarding and training

When asked if they had ever addressed these concerns with their managers, over 70% often said they had not. Many employees avoid having awkward conversations or lack the knowledge of when to have these discussions with their manager to address their concerns.[5] If you avoid hard conversations at work, you're not alone - many do.

Career progression is a process that can be easily managed with proper knowledge. Many employees hope concerns or issues get resolved by themselves, but that rarely happens. By actively engaging in the process, taking ownership, and applying the insights from this book, you'll reap the benefits and build a solid foundation for long-term career growth.

How To Use This Book

This book is designed to be your personal guide for mastering career progression strategies, combining data, insights, and real-life stories into a comprehensive approach. Each chapter explores a specific aspect of the Employee Lifecycle, offering actionable advice and practical steps, such as adopting the 'Let's Be Bullish' mindset, to support you on your career journey. For the best results, I recommend reading the book from start to finish. However, if you've already excelled in certain areas, feel free to jump forward and backward to different sections of the book that best meet your immediate needs.

After spending many years recruiting and hiring new college graduates and seeing them struggle to transition from college to the workplace, I wrote this book to share strategies and insights about the inner workings of an organization that can make a significant difference starting on day zero. My hope is that you find the guidance here transformative in your early days as a professional and that it lasts a lifetime.

This book is divided into four main parts, each designed to serve as a playbook you can apply and learn from throughout your career progression. Whether you're just starting your career as a new college graduate or advancing as an early-career professional, the strategies and advice provided are meant to guide you every step of the way. You'll find practical tips, real-life examples, and actionable steps to enhance your career progression, build valuable connections, and develop the skills necessary to start your career path on the right foot.

Here's the framework:

- **Part One:** *"So It Begins,"* kicks off your career journey—leaving your student days behind and stepping into the professional world.

- **Part Two:** *"The New World,"* focuses on accelerating your learning curve and career development in this new stage of your professional career.

- **Part Three:** *"Earn Your Wings,"* explores performance evaluation processes, addressing performance issues proactively, and understanding compensation strategies.

- **Part Four:** *"Path Unlocked,"* highlights evaluating personal value, career alignment, and professional relationships as you advance.

After each part, you'll find a dedicated 'Key Takeaways' page where you can write notes and actions you consider important based on your reading. This will help you remember key points and put your learnings into practice. Additionally, you'll encounter self-assessment and reflection prompts designed to deepen your understanding and application of the material.

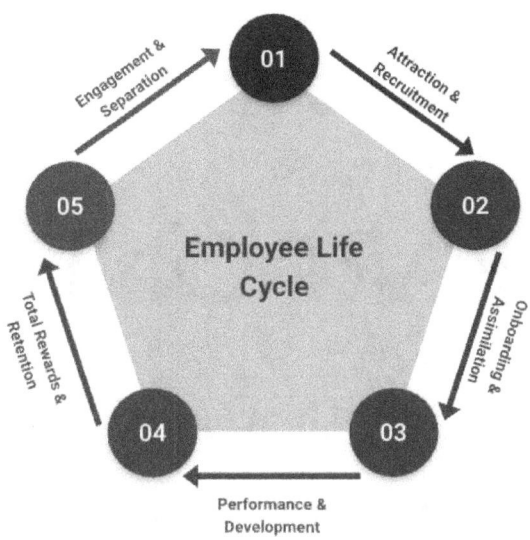

Figure 0.3: Typical Employee Lifecycle

By the end of this book, you'll have a comprehensive playbook that equips you with insights, tools, and stories for career excellence, covering foundational skills to navigating transitions across the Employee Lifecycle (see **Figure 0.3**).

These stages provide a comprehensive guide for your professional journey step by step. I invite you to fully engage with the material, apply the strategies, and work towards developing yourself into a successful early-career professional. Be proactive and assertive—take charge of your own development and make the most of your *"Zero to Three"* career progression. **In other words, be bullish.**

– Edward

PART ONE

SO, IT BEGINS

"The journey starts here"

1

CHAPTER

THE BIG LEAGUES

Congratulations—you made it! Landing your first job after college is no small feat. But here's the truth: now the real game begins. You're no longer just preparing—you're in it. This is your entry into the big leagues.

But remember, reaching this milestone is just the beginning. To truly make the most of this opportunity, it's crucial to carefully plan your next steps and start your new job on the right foot.

The weeks leading up to your first day might feel like Christmas. You're eagerly anticipating your start date while being showered with welcome gifts from the company. You might receive a "New Hire Welcome Kit" filled with company swag, a laptop, or other essentials. This kit is designed to make a positive first impression and help you feel like part of the team from day one.

As part of the onboarding process, expect to complete various forms, such as the I-9, tax documents, benefits enrollment, emergency contacts, and company policies. These are often done electronically but may be paper-based depending on the company. It might feel like a paperwork marathon—but trust me, it's just the warm up lap.

Make sure you understand what's needed ahead of time and bring any required documents to avoid delays. **Figure 1.1** outlines a typical onboarding process that new hires can expect.

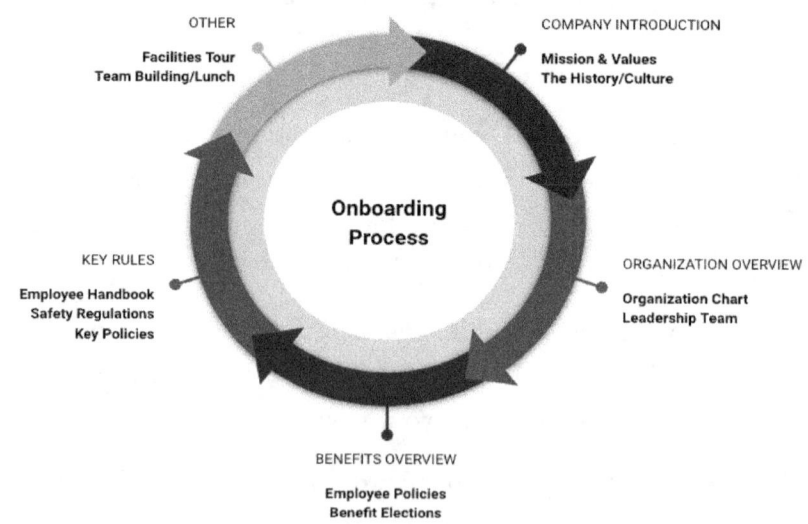

Figure 1.1: Typical Onboarding Model

During your first week, you'll likely participate in a New Hire Orientation that covers the company's mission, values, leadership, and strategy. Some orientations last a few hours; others may span a full week. You'll learn about workplace norms, systems, and possibly employee perks like meal subsidies, gym access, or career development programs. (see **Figure 1.1**).

This visual illustrates how many companies structure onboarding to support new hire assimilation during the first weeks of employment.

⚲AN INSIDER'S VIEW 🔎

From a company's perspective, onboarding is one of the most critical steps in the hiring process. It sets the tone for your experience and provides you with the tools and information you need to hit the ground running. Companies aim to make onboarding smooth, engaging, and productive to help new hires assimilate quickly and contribute confidently.

Here are a few best practices companies follow:

Pre-Start Communication:

Preparing well in advance is the best way to ensure a smooth first day for you as the new hire. Companies usually begin onboarding at least one to two weeks before the start date. During this time, they'll coordinate systems access, equipment, and notify security and IT—so you're not scrambling on Day Zero.

Next, companies may email you with all the information you'll need for your first day, including arrival time (or Zoom invites if the role is remote), parking information, or instructions on where to go when they enter the building. They may also share an agenda for the first day so that you know what to expect. Additionally, they'll normally provide a contact person so you'll know who to reach should you have any questions or concerns.

By communicating with you ahead of time, companies will make a positive first impression and ease any anxiety or apprehension you may feel about starting your new job.

Workspace Setup:

Setting up equipment for an employee workstation can be time-consuming and delay your training or familiarization with their systems. To avoid this, companies usually will start the setup process well before you arrive. The company should ask you about their equipment preferences, such as whether you prefer a MacBook or a PC. Providing this choice is to show that they want you to feel comfortable in the new setting.

The company should ensure all equipment is fully functional and ready to use and provide all necessary passwords and login information so you can get started without any unexpected technology delays.

Companies may add a few special touches by furnishing your workspace with new office supplies (e.g. an "office starter kit") and including swag or branded gifts, such as coffee mugs, t-shirts, notebooks, and other items. Companies love to give new hires swag so they can share it on their social channels to promote their new beginnings. These gestures can help you feel recognized and appreciated when they arrive.

Meet The Executives:

Involving a CEO or top executives in the onboarding program is one of the best ways to create a work environment that engages new hires and strengthens their connection with the organization and its goals. Executive participation demonstrates the value placed on the entire workforce, boosting morale and fostering a sense of pride and camaraderie among new employees.

For new hires, meeting the company's top leaders and hearing updates on company performance, strategic initiatives, and upcoming challenges provides valuable insights. As you better understand the company's direction, you're more likely to feel invested and motivated to contribute to its success. More importantly, these sessions foster open communication, allowing you to share your thoughts, ideas, and concerns directly with executives. Such personal interactions humanize the leadership team, making them more approachable and relatable to the workforce.

New Hire Announcements:

Introducing a new hire to everyone in a larger organization is rarely feasible, but it's still important to let people know a new team member has arrived. Sending a new employee announcement via email or Slack is one of the best onboarding practices, as it helps others become familiar with new hires and fosters new working relationships.

The announcement should include the new hire's name, job title, key responsibilities, and academic and professional background.

It should also highlight some fun facts that can act as conversation starters with other employees, such as their hobbies, unique talents, or favorite sports teams. Including a solo photo or pictures from a recent trip, family, or pet can also help others recognize and greet the new hire.

Depending on your organization's size, you may send this announcement to everyone or those working directly with the new hire.

Group Orientation:

A new hire orientation program is an excellent opportunity to communicate the company's mission, vision, and values and introduce their new employees to the company culture. This is also the time for you to complete necessary paperwork and ask questions about your benefits package and the organization's policies and procedures. Given the large amount of information to cover, it's often more efficient to hold these sessions with several new hires at once rather than in individual one-on-one meetings.

Pair New Employees with A Peer Mentor:

To help you assimilate and ensure you have a point of contact for guidance during their first few weeks, they'll normally pair you with a "buddy." This person should be at a similar level and have a similar role, acting as your mentor throughout the training process.

An experienced peer can provide valuable knowledge and advice, introduce you to essential contacts within the organization, and show you around the facility. Because the peer mentor is at the same professional level, you're likely to feel more comfortable asking questions and sharing uncertainties than with someone in a more senior leadership position.

Orientation isn't just about company trivia and swag—it's your first credibility test. Are you engaged? Are you asking good questions? The impression you make here shapes how seriously people take you going forward.

THE EMPLOYEE LIFECYCLE

As mentioned earlier, companies invest significant time and effort to make new hires feel welcome and part of the organization from the start. This marks the beginning of the Employee Lifecycle (see **Figure 1.2**), an HR model that captures the different stages of an employee's journey. Although the specifics of this model vary between companies and industries, many elements are consistent. It encompasses the idea that a new hire will go through distinct stages during their employee experience: before, during, and after employment.

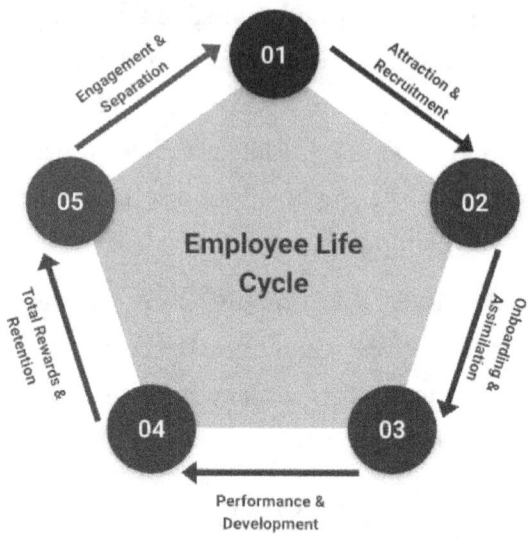

Figure 1.2: Typical Employee Lifecycle

Some companies use a more comprehensive cycle with many stages, while others may combine stages to create a smaller cycle. The exact components of each stage may also vary for each organization and its unique culture.

What does this mean for you?

As a new hire, you have successfully completed the first stage of the Employee Lifecycle: "Attraction & Recruitment." This was the phase of job searches, interviews, and ultimately receiving an offer. Although it was undoubtedly grueling, you persevered and accepted the offer. Now, during the second stage, "Onboarding & Assimilation," your task is to gain as much knowledge about the organization, the team, and your role as possible so that you can quickly contribute.

This stage marks the beginning of your transition from candidate to new hire. Companies strive to share enough information so that you, as the new hire, understand the company's goals, attitudes, and values. They also want you to recognize the role you'll play in helping build and support the organization.

While you might think the job interview ends once you accept the offer, the reality is different: , you're still being assessed—and often with more scrutiny. As the "new employee," people across the organization will be watching how you show up, how you learn, and how quickly you adapt. The spotlight is on you, even if you don't realize it. The first 90 days aren't a grace period—they're a high-stakes audition.

Here are some questions your new peers or colleagues may be asking or considering as you start with the company:

- "Did the new hire show up?"
- "How's the new hire doing so far?"
- "Is this who we hired for the role?"
- "What's the new hire like?"
- "What's their background?"
- "What projects will this new hire work on?"

When someone new joins a team, there's a natural curiosity. As a new hire, you'll be closely observed by others—consciously or not. They'll be sizing up how well you fit into the team, how quickly you absorb new information, and how open you are to coaching. Many new hires underestimate this quiet scrutiny and take a more passive approach to integrating. Don't miss your window to show your value early—because whether you realize it or not, people are paying attention.

LENNOX'S STORY

Support Changes Everything

Lennox, a senior manager, leads a team of technical support engineers. Just a few months into hiring Milani's new role, he contacted me as his HR Business Partner to discuss her progress.

During our meeting, Lennox said, "I think I have an issue." When I asked what the concern was, he explained, "Milani isn't picking things up as well as she should. When I address this with her, she doesn't ask questions, so I can't identify the problem or why she isn't grasping the training we are providing her."

Based on Milani's initial performance, Lennox felt he might have made the wrong hiring decision and considered letting her go. I gave Lennox several options to explore before making a final decision. I reminded him that Milani was an entry-level employee who needed adequate support to ramp up. I also suggested assigning her a mentor within the team so she could receive guidance and coaching from a more senior team member.

I strongly emphasized that Lennox should speak to her as soon as possible since she struggled to meet expectations.

A few weeks later, I reconnected with Lennox to check on Milani's progress. He shared, "She's doing better, and having her work with her mentor, Stefan, helped her fully grasp the concepts of her role." The one-on-one coaching sessions enabled Milani to understand the organization's goals, KPIs, and software tools. However, Lennox noted that Milani remained a bit timid in group settings and hoped she would gain more confidence over time and become more vocal in team stand-up sessions.

Overall, Lennox felt Milani was progressing well and on the right track now that he understood where she needed more development. He ensured Milani knew where her performance needed improvement. He took the time to get to know her better, learning how she best absorbs new concepts and identifying any barriers to satisfactory performance.

If you're an HR professional, Lennox's story may feel all too familiar. Managers often form quick opinions about new hires—sometimes before they've had a real chance to perform. That's the reality many early-career employees walk into.

As a recent graduate, you may have just earned your degree—but you were hired for your potential, not your experience. What does that mean? It means your future promise mattered more than your résumé. Companies who hire for potential are looking for people who are eager to learn, adaptable, and aligned with their values—even if you haven't had a chance to prove yourself yet.

So now it's time to prove them right.

To do that, you'll need to understand how your strengths translate into the workplace. A good place to start? Look at the core performance competencies companies use to evaluate success. These are the habits and behaviors you'll want to develop early—and consistently demonstrate.

CORE PERFORMANCE COMPETENCIES

Companies often evaluate new hires based on observable behaviors known as performance competencies—the building blocks of professional success. These common competencies aren't just buzzwords—they're real-world skills you'll be expected to demonstrate early and often (see **Table 1.3**).[6]

Competency	What It Looks Like in Action
Communication	Speak clearly, write professionally, and listen actively in all formats.
Analytical Thinking	Break down problems, think critically, and propose smart, thoughtful solutions.
Teamwork	Collaborate effectively, contribute to group goals, and support team dynamics.
Innovation	Offer creative ideas, improve processes, or challenge "how it's always been done."

Initiative	Volunteer for tasks, look for ways to help, and act before being asked.
Accountability	Follow through, take ownership of mistakes, and deliver results consistently.
Adaptability	Stay flexible under pressure, pivot when priorities shift, and stay calm during change.

Table 1.3: Core Performance Competencies

These competencies aren't theoretical—they're what managers and teammates notice, talk about, and remember. They're the traits that separate someone who just shows up from someone who gets noticed. More importantly, these behaviors shape how your manager and team see you—and they help you build credibility fast.

You dazzled during your interviews. Now that you're on the team, it's time to build on that momentum. The same traits that helped you land the job—curiosity, drive, professionalism—are what will carry you through your first year. Keep showing up with confidence, keep learning, and keep demonstrating that hiring you was the right decision.

♈ Let's Be Bullish:

Suppose your company does not provide an agenda or itinerary for the first few days after your start date. In that case, I recommend using a new hire checklist as a tool, as shown in **Table 1.4**, to create your own customized onboarding experience for yourself. Consider this checklist as your guide from the first day on the job through the first few months.

This checklist provides a quick roadmap as you assimilate into your new environment. This checklist is intentionally simple—it's designed to help you integrate into your role, your team, and the broader organization.

The focus is on acquiring the necessary knowledge, skills, and resources to perform your job effectively. Your onboarding should include ongoing training, mentoring, and continuous feedback to ensure you become a productive and engaged team member.

DONE	TASK	WHEN
✓	**Welcome and Orientation**	**Day 1**
	Meet Other New Hires (network)	Day 1
	In-Office: Tour the workspace and office areas: • Break room and lunch area • Conference Rooms • Restrooms	Day 1

	• Emergency Exit Plan • Gym	
	Complete New Hire Paperwork: • 1-9 form (employment eligibility) • W-4 form • Direct Deposit form • Emergency Contacts	Day 1
	Access & Set-up • Employee Handbook • Department Org Chart • Login instructions/Network	Day 1
	Schedule time with the manager to review: • Job Description/Expectations • Key Initiatives • Project Assignments and deadlines	Day 1-2
	First Two Weeks: Training and Review	
	Have one-on-one meetings with key employees; ensure daily meetings with peer mentors and project leaders are scheduled.	Day 3-5
	Review the org chart and company	Day 3-5

	structure; share who does what.	
	Shadow a peer for the day to see what a typical workday looks like.	Day 3-5
	Take training on software systems and other job tools.	Day 3-5
	Schedule a meeting at the end of the first week with the manager to check the progress.	Day 3-5
	Meet with HR to identify needs, concerns, issues, or ideas.	Day 7-14
	Additional Tasks and Notes	

Table 1.4: New Hire Checklist Template

UNDERSTANDING IMPOSTER SYNDROME

Let me address an increasingly prevalent topic among people transitioning to a new environment: imposter syndrome. This psychological pattern involves individuals doubting their accomplishments and persistently fearing they will be exposed as frauds, despite clear evidence of their competence and success.[7]

This phenomenon is particularly common among high achievers, who often attribute their success to luck or external factors rather than their own abilities. New hires, in particular, may experience imposter syndrome as they navigate their new roles and environments, feeling unworthy of their position or fearing they will not live up to expectations.

As a Human Resources Executive, I often work with employees who have been promoted into new roles or new hires who experience feelings of imposter syndrome when stepping into a new position, particularly in a competitive or high-performing environment. Despite their qualifications and the achievements that led to their hiring, they might feel unworthy of their position and fear being exposed as incapable or fraudulent.

These feelings can be exacerbated by the pressure to prove themselves, the need to quickly adapt to new responsibilities, and the presence of experienced colleagues. This internal struggle can lead them to question their abilities, attributing their success to luck or external factors rather than their own skills and hard work.

If you find yourself experiencing imposter syndrome while adjusting to your new role, here are some tips to help you cope:[8]

1. **Acknowledge Your Feelings**

   The first step in overcoming imposter syndrome is acknowledging and understanding your feelings. Recognize that these doubts and fears are common and do not reflect your abilities or worth. By identifying these thoughts, you can begin to challenge and reframe them.

2. Focus on Your Strengths

Take time to reflect on your skills, accomplishments, and the qualities that earned you your position. Make a list of your achievements and refer to it whenever you feel like an imposter. This practice can help reinforce your confidence and remind you of your capabilities.

3. Seek Support

Talking to colleagues, mentors, or friends about your feelings can provide reassurance and perspective. You may find that others have experienced similar doubts and can offer valuable advice on how they overcame them. Building a support network within your workplace can also create a sense of belonging and reduce feelings of isolation.

4. Set Realistic Goals

Set achievable goals for yourself and celebrate your progress. Break down tasks into manageable steps and recognize each small success. This approach can help you build confidence gradually and reduce the pressure to perform perfectly from the outset.

5. Embrace Mistakes as Learning Opportunities

Understand that making mistakes is a natural part of the learning process. Instead of viewing errors as evidence of inadequacy, see them as opportunities for growth and improvement. Reflect on what you can learn from each experience and how it can contribute to your development.

6. Practice Self-Compassion

Be kind to yourself and practice self-compassion. Treat yourself with the same understanding and patience you would offer a friend. Remember that everyone, including those you admire, experiences self-doubt at times.

7. Seek Professional Development

Take advantage of training and development opportunities offered by your company. Building new skills and expanding your knowledge can boost your confidence and competence in your role. Continuous learning helps reinforce that you are capable and equipped to handle your responsibilities.

8. Visualize Success

Use visualization techniques to imagine yourself succeeding in your role. Picture yourself confidently handling tasks, contributing to meetings, and achieving your goals. Visualization can create a positive mindset and increase your self-assurance.

9. Give Yourself Time

Adjusting to a new role takes time. Allow yourself the grace to learn and grow into your position. Recognize that it's normal to take some time to feel fully confident and competent in a new job.

By understanding and addressing imposter syndrome, you can navigate your new role with greater confidence and ease. Remember, your organization hired you for a reason, and you have the potential to succeed. Embrace the opportunities ahead, trust in your abilities, and be open to learning and growth.

Imposter syndrome can affect many new employees, especially in competitive industries where expectations are high. It's important to recognize that feeling uncertain or doubting your abilities is normal, particularly when starting in a new role or environment. Yet, acknowledging these feelings and actively challenging them can lead to personal growth and professional success. Seek out mentors or peers who can provide perspective and support and remember that growth often comes from stepping outside your comfort zone. By gradually expanding your skills and knowledge, you'll not only overcome imposter syndrome but also thrive in your role over time.

Imposter syndrome is a common experience that can affect individuals at any stage of their career. It's important to recognize that these feelings are normal and can often be overcome with time and effort. Remember, everyone starts somewhere, and learning and growth are continuous processes.

Embrace the challenges and opportunities that come your way and use them as stepping stones to build confidence and competence in your role. Stay open to feedback, remain curious, and take pride in your progress—no matter how small. By cultivating a growth mindset and focusing on your strengths, you'll navigate your career path with greater resilience and clarity.

You were hired because someone saw potential in you—don't forget that. You belong here. Keep learning. Keep growing.

BULLISH PRO TIPS

- **Own your onboarding.** Don't assume the company has it all figured out—use a personal checklist to stay on track.

- **You're still being interviewed.** First impressions extend beyond Day 1. People are watching—show up strong.

- **Ask for a peer buddy.** If your company doesn't assign one, be proactive and request someone who can guide you.

- **Understand your role's impact.** Get clarity on how your job contributes to the company's mission and success.

- **Fight imposter syndrome with facts.** Keep a "Ta-Da" list of wins and positive feedback to remind yourself you belong.

Don't sit back waiting to be molded. Be bold, be present, show them why you were the right hire. That's how you start strong. That's how you be bullish.

Closing Reflection:

Starting your first job can feel overwhelming, but those early doubts are part of the journey. The real test comes as you step into a team—and learn how to build your foundation there.

Let's Recap!

- **Onboarding Momentum**: The transition from candidate to new hire is critical. A strong onboarding process helps you maintain the positive momentum you built during interviews.

- **Understand the Employee Lifecycle**: Get familiar with your company's Employee Lifecycle model so you can better navigate your growth journey from day one.

- **Prepare for Your First Day**: Show up focused and ready—your first interactions matter, and your new colleagues will be watching.

- **Demonstrate Your Potential**: You were hired for your promise, not just your past. Embrace this as your opportunity to grow and shine.

- **Use an Onboarding Checklist**: A structured checklist can help you stay organized and make sure nothing falls through the cracks during your first few weeks.

- **Address Imposter Syndrome**: It's normal to feel self-doubt. Acknowledge it, work through it, and let your confidence grow with every win.

Above all, remember: How you start matters. Show up, speak up, and be bullish.

2

CHAPTER

LAY THE FOUNDATION

When you join a new team, there's more to figure out than your job description. Every team has its rhythm—how they communicate, collaborate, make decisions, and support one another. This is often called the "Ways of Working" or "WoW." I first came across the term years ago, and it stuck with me. WoW isn't just a process—it's the invisible playbook that can make or break your success.[9]

In simpler terms, WoW is how a team works together. While ways of working differ from organization to organization, there are core elements that teams should strive to include. These expectations serve as ground rules and keep everyone aligned.

As a new hire, you might experience onboarding where assimilation is highly structured and comprehensive. You might receive a checklist that outlines meetings, rituals, and team processes. You're introduced to each meeting's purpose, provided with agendas and summaries, and connected to team members who walk you through workflows and internal systems. These thoughtful touches can go a long way in making you feel welcomed and included from the very start.

But not every company operates this way. Some—especially startups—prefer an ad hoc, fast-moving culture. These environments pride themselves on agility, often zigging while others zag—but that pace, while exciting, can also overwhelm new hires. Without a clear onboarding process, your ramp-up period may be delayed, and it's not uncommon to feel disconnected or unsure of your role. Many new grads in these situations experience "buyer's remorse"—a dip in enthusiasm after the initial high of receiving the offer.

THE IMPORTANCE OF WAYS OF WORKING

As you start your career and integrate into your team, pay close attention to how the group functions. Understand how objectives are established, how communication flows, how team rules are designed, and how internal problems are resolved.[10] Observe how team members encourage one another to adhere to the team's ways of working to achieve goals, increase collaboration, enhance productivity, and improve overall effectiveness and project performance.

To establish the team's ways of working, it is necessary to identify the procedures, standards, and principles that guide how a team functions and collaborates:

1. **Define the Team's Goals:** Clarify what the team is trying to achieve.

2. **Assign Tasks and Responsibilities**: Ensure it is clear who is in charge of which tasks and deliverables.

3. **Outline the Decision-Making Process**: Explain how the team will make decisions. Outline the steps involved and who has the authority to make final decisions.

4. **Establish Timeline and Milestones**: Develop a schedule with specific deadlines and checkpoints to track progress.

5. **Onboarding and Training**: Provide training and onboarding materials to new team members to help them quickly understand and adopt the team's norms.

6. **Evaluate and Adjust**: Regularly evaluate the team's alignment with its WOW and refine where needed.

To see how things can quietly unravel when onboarding falls short, let me introduce you to Rachel.

RACHEL'S STORY

When Silence Backfires

Rachel was a recent graduate hired as a Customer Success Specialist, reporting to Milo, a manager of the customer solutions organization. This team focuses on post-sales management and maintains strategic relationships with small and medium-sized customers. After just three months, Rachel resigned unexpectedly.

In Rachel's exit interview, she shared that she felt like she didn't belong. "The rest of the CS (Customer Success) team was really tight knit. They'd worked together for a long time," she said. "From day one, I felt like an outsider." She'd also heard a rumor that she was hired to fill in for someone on maternity leave—and that the team hoped that person would return. "It made me feel like a placeholder," she said. "I didn't get much training, and most days I had no idea what I was doing. Customers were upset. I didn't feel like I belonged."

Rachel added, "I don't think I'm a bad employee. I just never had a chance to show what I could do. That's why I'm leaving." When asked if she ever brought this up with her manager, she replied, "No. I didn't want him to think I was incapable."

When I debriefed Milo, he was surprised. He shared that Rachel was hired for her customer service experience in retail and believed she would do well with challenging customers. "Every time I asked how she was doing, she said 'okay,'" he told me. "I asked if she needed anything, and she always said 'no.'"

I informed Milo that Rachel thought she was hired to replace someone on the team who is currently out on maternity leave. He was dumbfounded. "Where did she hear that?" he asked. He clarified that this was not true. "She was hired because the team needed additional resources to drive customer retention and meet revenue goals. Rachel was part of our expansion strategy to improve our overall NPS scores," he explained.

Milo added that he was about to give Rachel her three-month performance review, highlighting the positive aspects of her work, areas that she was doing well, and customer feedback expressing their appreciation for her responsiveness. "I had no idea she was struggling," he admitted.

Rachel's story isn't uncommon. Without structured feedback or clear communication, it's easy to misread how you're doing. If you sense warning signs or feel you're falling short, discussing this with your manager or assigned buddy is essential. In Rachel's case, having regular check-ins could have allowed her to express, "I'm struggling and need more guidance."

As a new hire, if you notice any signs that you might be underperforming, it's essential to discuss them openly with your manager. This is the opportunity to ask, *"Am I meeting your expectations?"* Together, you can identify any necessary additional training or support. After implementing these adjustments, allow a few weeks to assess further progress.

In the first month, depending on the job, you might have a few indicators of your performance. For particularly complicated roles, this period might be longer. For simpler roles, you should be up and running within the first month. Ideally, you'll have a sense of how long it takes to get up to speed by working closely with your manager or assigned buddy.

If your company has a six-month probation period—which is common in many industries—don't wait until the end to check in. Request a midpoint review. You'll get a clear sense of what's working, where to focus your efforts, and how to course-correct if needed.

Treat these reviews as two-way conversations. Prepare a self-assessment and be honest about your experience. Here are some questions to guide you:

- What parts of the role am I doing well in?
- Where do I feel lost or need more training?
- Are there any blockers affecting my work?
- Do I understand the expectations and goals of my position?
- What feedback have I received, and how have I applied it?

The critical part of this process is the performance conversation you'll have. It's beneficial to set up a formal meeting in person or via Zoom dedicated solely to this performance feedback topic. This way, it won't be overshadowed by other agenda items, providing a focused time to discuss what's going well and what areas need improvement.

If there are areas where you're falling short, this is your opportunity to realign—with support and honest feedback guiding the way. Collaborate with your manager to pinpoint specific improvements and outline the support needed to achieve them. Structuring these discussions allows for immediate feedback, facilitates necessary adjustments, and sheds light on any hurdles you encounter. This approach empowers you to move forward decisively rather than contemplating a premature resignation.

⚲AN INSIDER'S VIEW ⚲

As you're laying your foundation, it's also smart to be aware of career pitfalls that can undermine your momentum. As a new hire, you have the chance to lay the groundwork for your professional career from the ground up. In light of this, I'd like to explain the concept of being considered a 'job hopper' so you can avoid this as you begin your journey as a newly minted professional.

In simple terms, a job hopper is someone whose résumé or LinkedIn shows frequent short stints—usually under a year—across multiple roles. While some career influencers claim the stigma is outdated, I can tell you from firsthand experience: hiring managers still pay attention to it.

How You Work Is Who You Become

As a Talent Acquisition Executive, I notice that this subject is rarely addressed from an internal recruiter's perspective, especially for recent graduates who are just establishing their professional careers. Although some so-called career experts may argue it's no longer relevant or is an old-fashioned view, from my experience partnering with hiring managers when interviewing roles at different levels, this continues to be viewed as a 'red flag' and unfavorable. I've had numerous conversations and debates with them when reviewing a questionable resume or LinkedIn profile, which often lead to extensive dialogue and interpretation about a candidate's job history.

When hiring managers observe this pattern of frequent job changes, they may infer either frequent dismissals or a tendency to leave jobs due to a lack of job satisfaction or engagement. While each job change usually has its own story, the overall impression remains clear: a resume that suggests job hopping signals a warning to hiring managers and perhaps avoid hiring this candidate altogether. It is challenging for hiring managers to assess a person's performance in roles that lasted less than two years.

According to a study, over 22% of workers aged 20 and older spent a year or less at their jobs in 2022—the highest percentage with such short tenure since 2006.[11] Strategic job changes for valid reasons can enhance your career. However, suppose these changes create doubt with decision-makers or require you to explain yourself as a candidate constantly. In that case, you're already in a position of uncertainty, or it puts a question mark on your candidacy for future roles.

Instead, maximize your role at your current company to the point where you must seek new opportunities to further your growth and development as the next step in your career progression.

Here are signs that might indicate someone is a job hopper:

- You've had more than five jobs at more than two companies within seven years.
- You have never spent more than a year in the same role.
- You start looking for a new job after being in your current role for less than three months.
- You have multiple gaps in your employment history that are not accounted for.
- The bullet points on your resume do not demonstrate skill growth, career progression, or business results.
- You frequently cite vague or generic reasons for leaving previous positions, such as 'seeking new challenges' without further explanation.
- Your LinkedIn profile shows numerous job updates within a short time frame.
- Backchannel References from former colleagues or managers frequently describe your departures as unexpected or abrupt.

If you're feeling stuck in your current job, consider talking to your manager about taking on new projects, seeking opportunities for skill development, or exploring other ways to make your current role more fulfilling.

In many cases, effective communication with your manager can lead to meaningful changes in your job that better align with your career goals and aspirations.

🐂 Let's Be Bullish:

Before deciding to leave your current organization, ask yourself, *"Why do I want to leave my current job? Is there a compelling reason?"* Suppose you are interviewing for your next role; you want to be in a favorable position to showcase and tell amazing stories about all of your accomplishments and the contributions you've made in your current position over the last three years. This will make you stand out as a strong candidate for new opportunities.

It's easy to panic when a role doesn't feel like the right fit right away. But with structure, feedback, and smart planning, you can take control of your career path—even in uncertain environments. Here's how to stay bullish when the ground feels shaky.

Here's how to avoid the job hopper label:

1. **Stay Longer in Each Role**

   - Showcase Reliability: To demonstrate commitment and stability, try to stay in each position for at least two years and focus on key deliverables during this time.

   - Evaluate Before Leaving: Before moving on to a new opportunity, ensure you have thoroughly evaluated your current job and exhausted growth opportunities.

2. Seek Growth Opportunities Internally

- Internal Transfers: Look for opportunities to grow within your current organization through promotions or lateral moves that provide new challenges and responsibilities.

- Professional Development: Take advantage of online training, certifications, and other professional development opportunities your employer offers.

3. Provide Clear Reasons for Job Changes

- Transparent Communication: Be prepared to explain your job changes clearly and succinctly. Focus on the positive aspects, such as career growth, skill development, or personal circumstances.

- Avoid Negativity: Remember to badmouth previous employers or roles when explaining your job changes.

4. Build a Cohesive Career Narrative

- Align Your Moves: Ensure each job change fits into a broader career plan and contributes to a coherent career narrative.

- Show Progression: Highlight how each role has contributed to your professional growth and prepared you for the next step.

5. Focus on Skill Development

- Highlight Achievements: Ensure your resume and LinkedIn profile highlight skills, achievements, and contributions in each role.

- Continuous Learning: Engage in constant learning to demonstrate your commitment to professional growth and development.

6. Avoid Impulsive Decisions

- Strategic Planning: Avoid leaving jobs impulsively. Take time to assess new opportunities and make strategic career moves.

- Resolve Issues: Attempt to resolve conflicts or dissatisfaction at your current job before deciding to leave.

7. Be Selective with your Next Job Search

- Targeted Applications: Apply for positions that align with your skills, experience, and long-term career goals. Ideally, your next role would be viewed as the next logical next step.

- Quality over Quantity: Focus on quality applications to roles with a strong fit rather than applying broadly to see what you can get.

8. Network and Seek Mentorship

- Build Relationships: Networking can provide insights into company culture and opportunities for internal growth.

- Seek Mentorship: A mentor at your current company who can provide guidance on making strategic career decisions and avoiding the pitfalls of job hopping.

9. Show Commitment in Other Ways

- Volunteer Work: Engage in long-term volunteer work or side projects that show commitment and dedication.

- Professional Organizations: Join and participate in professional organizations related to your field.

Why am I sharing this with you before starting your career journey? I want you to be more methodical when making career decisions early in your professional path. For hiring managers and recruiters, there's still an expectation that a candidate needs 3-5 years in a full-time job to make a significant impact and progress to the next level. Anything less can raise doubts. It's not fair—but it's real.

Why This Matters

It's simple. Companies invest thousands of dollars and hundreds of hours in onboarding and training new employees. If there's a risk that you won't stay, they're less likely to make that investment or even hire you. This can make you look "unserious" at best or a "problem employee" at worst, even if you've just had a string of bad luck. As you start your professional career, be aware of this narrative and strive to avoid it.

In my first book, *Be Bullish 101,* I cover the concept of "Backward Planning" related to job hunting. This strategy also applies to starting your career on the right foot. It involves envisioning your next big step, such as a promotion or next big career move, and then carefully plotting the steps to get there. Once you identify your goal, you can work backward to make decisions that align with and prepare you for your career path, starting from day zero in your current position.

This Backward Planning approach can help you make more informed decisions while establishing yourself as a new hire. It allows you to explore your areas of interest with greater focus. With this awareness and understanding of the stigma around job hopping—you can position yourself as a committed, strategic professional who isn't just chasing job titles, but building a meaningful career.

BULLISH PRO TIPS

- **Observe how your team works.** Ways of Working (WoW) tells you everything about how to thrive—or fail—on a team.

- **Initiate a performance conversation.** Don't wait six months to ask, "How am I doing?" Start that dialogue early.

- **Avoid being a job hopper.** Stick around long enough to tell a compelling story of contribution and growth.

- **Use backward planning.** Visualize where you want to be in 2–3 years and align your actions today with that future.

- **If you feel lost, say something.** Silent struggles only grow. Speak up before small issues become reasons to quit.

Closing Reflection:

A strong start depends on clarity, support, and teamwork. Once you find your place, the next challenge is proving yourself— showing you can handle the unknowns ahead of you.

Let's Recap!

- **Understanding Ways of Working:** Gaining insights into your organization's Ways of Working helps you grasp team ground rules and ensure alignment with team objectives.

- **Effective Integration:** Comprehending these guidelines enables you to better align your efforts with team goals, enhancing your integration and contribution to the team's success.

- **Adapting to Organizational Culture:** Understanding and adapting to the company's culture and values is crucial for fitting in and thriving. Demonstrating alignment with organizational norms and values can enhance your credibility and effectiveness.

- **Build Relationships:** Developing strong relationships with colleagues and stakeholders early on can significantly impact your success and integration within the team. Effective networking within the organization helps in understanding informal structures and gaining support from others.

- **Proactive Performance Reviews:** Requesting a performance review as a new hire demonstrates initiative, fosters clear communication, and sets you up for success within the organization.

- **Avoid Job Hopper Labels:** Stay long enough to add value and tell a compelling growth story.

- **Use Backward Planning:** Strategize your moves with your next big opportunity in mind.

You're not just building experience—you're laying the foundation for a reputation that will follow you into every room.

3

CHAPTER

———

EMBRACE THE UNKNOWN

Remember the days in grade school when a new kid was introduced to the class? Being the new kid at school can be a daunting and intimidating experience. It often feels like everyone else knows each other and exactly how to act. You might feel like you're invading a tight-knit group, nervous as you try to find your place. To fit in, you aim to make a great first impression, build friendships, and learn how things work.

Starting a new job as a recent hire mirrors that experience. There's usually a mix of excitement and anxiety—curiosity about the new environment paired with a desire to make a strong impression.

At this stage, you're still learning the ropes—but keep an eye out. Some of the best career moves you'll make might not be external job offers, but internal shifts you initiate once you're ready.

Orientation may include training on policies, introductions to coworkers and stakeholders, and guidance on how to navigate systems and workflows. Even with this support, adapting to the culture and social dynamics can be challenging.

New hires often grapple with feelings of overwhelm or imposter syndrome. That's why building relationships, asking for feedback, and seeking support from managers, mentors, and peers is critical. Over time, as you settle into your role and begin contributing meaningfully, you'll start to feel a greater sense of confidence and belonging.

Still, not all companies handle onboarding the same way. Some do it well. Others barely do it at all. The first 90 days are a highly impressionable period that shapes how new employees view the company, which impacts their long-term engagement, performance, and retention. So how do you take control of this early phase and make the most of your start?

The answer: a personal 90-day plan. Also known as a 30-60-90-day plan, it is a strategic roadmap designed by a new hire or hiring manager to guide new employees during their first three months. It outlines specific goals, tasks, and milestones for the new employee to achieve over the first 30, 60, and 90 days, ensuring they understand their role and responsibilities and can make meaningful contributions to the team and company.

Whether you're a new employee creating a plan during the interview process or a team leader crafting one for you as the new hire, a 90-day plan should set a clear roadmap of expectations. It also guides the new employee's actions for those first few months and help eliminate ambiguity and set clear direction.

1. **Setting Clear, Defined Goals:** These are the team or organization's expectations for the first 90 days, creating a roadmap for the new hire's initial steps in their position.

2. **Building Relationships:** Well-thought-out 90-day plans provide strategies and opportunities for establishing connections and trust within the organization or team, particularly among colleagues, managers, and stakeholders.

3. **Understanding the Organization:** Learning about the mission, values, culture, and processes of the organization is essential for employees to understand how they fit into the business's structure and goals, giving them a sense of purpose.

4. **Measuring Progress:** In addition to setting clear goals and expectations, there should be a clear way to track progress. This helps in determining feasible performance goals for the first three months, which can be adjusted as needed.

COMPONENTS OF AN EFFECTIVE 90-DAY PLAN

As a new hire, you might not yet be acquainted with the concept of a 90-Day plan (see **Table 3.1**). At a high-level, a 30-60-90-day plan typically outlines critical milestones for each month of onboarding. Let me explain further:

- **Days 0-30:** During this initial month, intensive training is prioritized to familiarize the new hire with company policies, products, team dynamics, and job responsibilities.

- **Days 31–60:** The second month focuses on applying the acquired knowledge through practical tasks. This phase encourages learning through hands-on experience, allowing room for errors as the new hire adjusts to workflows.

- **Days 61–90:** By the third month, the new hire should be proficient in their role, demonstrating mastery of skills and meeting job expectations effectively. This period marks the transition towards achieving long-term performance goals

See **Figure 3.1** for an example of a structured sales onboarding plan that includes goals, priorities, and metrics across each stage.

30 Days
FOCUS:

- Learn the company's mission, growth plan, and product.

GOALS:

- Develop knowledge of products, features, account types, and sales processes.

PRIORITIES:

- Complete product knowledge training, read & watch customer success stories, and work through new sales checklist.
- Participate in the Sales Boot Camp.

METRICS:

- Score 90% or higher on knowledge assessment and complete the required assignments.

60 Days

FOCUS:

- Gain three new accounts and work alongside cross-functional teams

GOALS:

- Manage three customer accounts and assist lead

representatives in technical support audit.

PRIORITIES:

- Complete role-playing scenarios, schedule 1-on-1 with the support lead, and learn about upcoming releases, and current projects.

METRICS:

- Complete the new customer journey assessment and have a 1-on-1 with my manager.

90 Days

FOCUS:

- Get prepared for Sales QBR and present audit findings.

GOALS:

- Deepen understanding of product knowledge and assist accounts with technical support.

PRIORITIES:

- Complete audit findings and customer interviews.
- Complete the features and technical support training

modules.
METRICS: • Gain 1-3 mid-level accounts and report new customers, and audit findings in team meetings.

Table 3.1: An example of a 90-Day Plan

Whether in your first week or your fourth, a strong 90-day plan keeps you not just running—but running in the right direction.

1. **Research & preparation**

    Creating an effective 30-60-90-day plan hinges on establishing a solid foundation of understanding. Skipping the crucial research and preparation stage can impede subsequent steps, such as goal setting and capability development, as new hires lack the necessary context to guide their actions.

    Begin by researching your company's culture, mission, and values. This foundational insight is important for aligning your plan with business priorities and clarifying how your role contributes to the team's overall strategy.

    Your research should also cover the position's job description, which helps outline core job responsibilities and expectations. This is an excellent opportunity to review this with your manager, so you are on the same page. Knowing this will help both you and your manager set, prioritize, and take action on goals. If there are things you're unsure about–like goals, expectations, or key priorities–ask! This is your opportunity to demonstrate curiosity and learn more about the organization.

2. Goal setting

When you know the context behind your 30-60-90-day plan, you can start identifying objectives.

What are the specific, concrete goals for the new hire to achieve in the first 90 days? These goals should be specific and concrete, tailored to your personal aspirations and performance metrics and aligned with the organization's broader objectives. It's essential to ensure these objectives are realistic within the given time frame—expecting to achieve significant milestones in the first week isn't feasible.

Consider employing various goal-setting methods such as SMART goals (see **Table 3.2**). SMART goals break down the goal-setting process into Specific, Measurable, Achievable, Relevant, and Time-bound increments, providing a structured pathway for advancing your career during the initial stages of your employment. Understanding how to develop SMART goals will be beneficial in the long run, especially when you begin using OKRs, which will be explained later in upcoming chapters.

S	Specific	What exactly are you trying to achieve?
M	Measurable	How will you know when you've achieved it?
A	Achievable	Is it genuinely possible to achieve it?
R	Relevant	Does it contribute to your organization's mission?
T	Time-Based	When do you want to achieve this by?

Table 3.2: Definition of SMART Goals

3. Action plan

You need to train to understand your new team's processes because, let's face it, starting a new job is being in a foreign environment. Your action plan is really just a set of guidelines telling you what you're going to do and by when.

Consider SMART goals once again. After defining your objective (the specific component), outline the steps required to accomplish it (the measurable component). These actions are tangible tasks that you can track and assess. In the context of a 90-day plan, think of this process as a strategic approach to training and integration.

If you need to understand team processes (remember WoW), your measurable action is studying relevant documentation.

Of course, no action plan is complete without a deadline. Saying your first 90-day plan goals have to be done within the first 90 days is a no-brainer, but that can be too broad, leaving you demotivated. So, it's more beneficial to break your main goal down into smaller components, each with its own deadline, to ensure that your development actions are on track for the first 90 days in your new job.

4. Relationship building

Almost every role within a company involves some level of interaction with various teams, making it vital for a 30-60-90-day plan to prioritize building relationships with key team members and stakeholders. Collaborating with your manager during this stage is invaluable for gaining input and a broader understanding of the organization's objectives.

A practical approach is to schedule dedicated time in your first 90-day plan for meetings with relevant stakeholders, team members, and colleagues. These sessions provide opportunities to introduce yourself, grasp their roles within the team's dynamics and processes, and understand their priorities.

It also builds early connections with key collaborators and gives you insight into how the team communicates, handles conflict, and works together—critical context for integrating effectively into the team structure.

5. Capability development

Entering a new job always presents learning opportunities because no one starts knowing everything. A well-crafted first 90-day plan should include a capability assessment to evaluate your current competencies and pinpoint gaps between what you know and what the job demands. This assessment also serves as immediate feedback on your progress thus far.

The goal of this plan isn't just to identify gaps but also to create pathways for improvement through targeted training. Opportunities for capability development include utilizing knowledge management systems or an LMS, engaging in formal training sessions, receiving formal and informal coaching, and participating in workshops or webinars.

For instance, imagine you've joined a sales team, and they have identified a beginner-level competence in product and industry knowledge. As part of your 30-60-90-day plan, arrange for a mentor to provide guidance and expertise. Additionally, schedule time within your plan for independent research to deepen your understanding of your role and industry landscape.

6. Continuous evaluation

Although called a 30-60-90-day plan, it shouldn't be discarded once the initial 90 days are over. By this point, you should be settled into your role and clearly understand your responsibilities and expectations.

It's essential to continuously evaluate and review the onboarding process throughout the 30-60-90-day plan rather than waiting until the end. Regular check-ins track your progress and gather valuable feedback from your manager or mentor.

The goal is to consistently assess your development and receive support from your manager to ensure success in your new role. While some may find it hard to brag about their accomplishments, showcasing your hard work is necessary. Therefore, schedule weekly one-on-one meetings with your manager throughout the process.

This regular cadence provides a consistent opportunity to connect, receive ongoing feedback, and adjust as needed. Use the 90-day plan as a guide and take pride in your progress. By doing so, you'll define your success and give visibility to your recent projects as you reflect on your achievements.

᛫AN INSIDER'S VIEW ᛫

WHAT IF YOU DON'T HAVE A 90-DAY PLAN?

A robust onboarding process is important for laying the groundwork for success as you transition into your new job. Without a well-defined 30-60-90-day plan designed in collaboration with your manager, you risk setting yourself up for challenges and potential setbacks.

What does this mean in practice? No one starts a new job fully equipped with all the necessary knowledge, expertise, and skills, especially in a new company where you also need to learn the culture and mission. These factors significantly impact the time it takes to achieve proficiency in your role.

A structured 30-60-90-day plan, including dedicated training, accelerates this proficiency timeline, ensuring you can contribute effectively sooner rather than later. Without such a plan, new hires find themselves struggling to integrate smoothly, relying heavily on team support, which can hinder both productivity and team morale. Moreover, the business misses out on potential value during the adjustment period.

Unclear expectations further complicate matters. Without a defined plan, you may struggle to understand your job description and responsibilities, making it difficult to set and achieve personal goals. This lack of clarity not only hampers professional and personal development but also prevents your skills and knowledge from aligning with the demands of your role. Inadequate training worsens these challenges, leading to knowledge gaps and an increased likelihood of errors.

Ultimately, these issues contribute to low employee engagement and high turnover, mainly if new hires don't receive the necessary support to acclimate to the company's culture and understand its mission. When employees leave prematurely, it imposes significant costs on the business for recruitment, hiring, and training replacements. It also disrupts team dynamics, lowers overall productivity, and diminishes the organization's overall value.

In essence, a well-executed 30-60-90-day plan not only accelerates job proficiency, but from a company perspective it also enhances employee satisfaction, reduces turnover, and optimizes business performance.

MAKE AN EARLY IMPRESSION

In the early stages, numerous opportunities will arise to observe and contribute to projects beyond your usual duties. Instead of clocking out or logging off, ask your manager if there's anything else you can assist with before you call it a day. Even if it means staying a bit longer, say 'yes' or 'let me try' at every opportunity. Demonstrating a willingness to learn proves your commitment to the company. It shows employers you have the drive, self-discipline, and motivation to enhance your skills and prepare for new challenges.

Hiring managers want new hires to be able to demonstrate that they can adapt to changing circumstances and environments and take on board new ideas and concepts. They want employees with the confidence to respond positively to change and new ways of working; employees who are prepared to rise to the challenge of dealing with the unfamiliar and show they can cope with the new or unexpected.

Here's a sample of actual phrasing from recent job postings:

- "A positive 'can do' attitude and a willingness to grasp opportunities."

- "We want you to demonstrate a dynamic approach."

- "We're after ambitious graduates who can respond with pace and energy"

- "We are looking for graduates with the right attitude to change."

These quotes are all taken from recent graduate job descriptions from various job boards. As you can see, they don't use the words 'adaptable' or 'flexible,' but these recruiters are looking for candidates who have these qualities. They want new hires who can thrive in a culture of change and continuous improvement and can be flexible in how they work and think.

TOM BRADY'S STORY

Prepared for the Moment

Whether or not you admire Tom Brady, his legendary NFL career, over two decades filled with record-breaking performances, offers invaluable insights into effective leadership. From a sixth-round draft pick to one of the greatest quarterbacks in history, Brady's journey exemplifies not only athletic excellence but also profound leadership qualities that transcend sports. His unwavering confidence sets him apart as a role model in leadership.

New England Patriots owner Robert Kraft recalls meeting Tom Brady for the first time when Brady was a 22-year-old newcomer to the organization. "I still have the image of Tom Brady coming down the old Foxboro stadium steps with that pizza box under his arm, a skinny beanpole. When he introduced himself to me and said, 'Hi, Mr. Kraft,' he was about to explain who he was, but I said, 'I know who you are, you're Tom Brady. You're our sixth-round draft choice,'" recalled Kraft. "And he looked me in the eye and said, 'I'm the best decision this organization has ever made.' It looks like he could be right."

Brady even told his high school coach, Tom MacKenzie, that if he ever got a chance to replace the starting quarterback, the Patriots would never take his job away. "Drew Bledsoe is such a talented quarterback, but I've got one advantage over him," Brady told MacKenzie. "I pay more attention to detail. ... If I ever get a chance to get that first-string job, nobody's taking it away from me."

Later that season, Brady led his team to his first Super Bowl appearance against the favored St. Louis Rams. In the locker room before Super Bowl XXXVI, Brady told third-stringer Damon Huard, "We'll know what it feels like to be world champions in three-and-a-half hours." Brady and his underdog team then upset the Rams and won the Super Bowl.[12]

Tom Brady's career offers more than a blueprint for sporting excellence; it provides valuable lessons in preparation, confidence, and leadership applicable to any field. His journey underscores the importance of resilience, preparation, adaptability, teamwork, self-care, and humility—qualities that define not only a great athlete but also a great leader.

Tom Brady's confidence during his rookie year stemmed from several key factors. His rigorous preparation and strong work ethic, including countless hours studying playbooks and honing his skills, gave him a deep understanding of the game and a competitive edge. Brady's mental toughness allowed him to stay focused and composed under pressure, contributing significantly to his self-assurance.

A strong support system of coaches, teammates, and mentors who believed in his potential provided encouragement and guidance, further bolstering his confidence. Additionally, his successful college career at the University of Michigan, where he overcame numerous challenges, prepared him for the professional level.

Tom Brady's growth mindset and unwavering determination to succeed fueled his belief in his abilities and commitment to continuous improvement. Overcoming setbacks, such as being a low draft pick and facing competition for his position, strengthened his determination and reinforced his confidence. These factors combined to create a foundation of confidence that Brady carried with him throughout his rookie year and beyond.

Research indicates that approximately 70% of employees lack self-confidence when speaking up at work, a factor that can significantly hinder their professional success. This lack of self-assurance can lead to missed opportunities, underutilized potential, and stunted career growth. Working professionals can draw inspiration from Tom Brady's remarkable self-confidence to overcome this challenge. By adopting his mindset and strategies, employees can build their confidence, effectively communicate their ideas, and ultimately achieve greater career success.

Here are some tips inspired by Tom Brady's approach to self-confidence:

- Recognize your strengths
- Have a positive attitude toward yourself
- Don't compare yourself to others
- Acquire skills in areas where you are lacking
- Seize the moment when an opportunity presents itself

As professionals, our journey toward success often involves a relentless pursuit of new opportunities that promise to elevate our careers to greater heights. In this pursuit, however, we may inadvertently overlook the wealth of opportunities surrounding us in our current roles and environments. By shifting our focus and perspective, we can realize that true growth and fulfillment come not only from reaching distant goals but also from fully embracing and maximizing the potential of the opportunities right in front of us.

These opportunities, whether they involve expanding our skills, building stronger relationships with colleagues, or taking on new responsibilities, serve as mere building blocks to realizing our full potential. Embracing these present opportunities enriches your professional journey and cultivates a mindset of continuous growth and development.

Like Tom Brady during this rookie year, seizing the moment when an opportunity presents itself is crucial, especially for new hires. Often, opportunities come in subtle forms, such as a chance to lead a project, offer input during a meeting, or volunteer for a new initiative. Recognizing and acting on these opportunities can set you apart and demonstrate your value to the organization. Don't hesitate to step out of your comfort zone; taking calculated risks can lead to significant rewards. When you seize these moments, you not only build your confidence but also showcase your proactive attitude and readiness to take on challenges, ultimately accelerating your career growth.

As you start your new job, remember that first impressions matter. Establishing a strong first impression sets the tone for your relationships with colleagues and manager. Be approachable, eager to learn, and willing to contribute. Volunteer for tasks and projects, even if they are outside your immediate job description. This willingness to go above and beyond shows your commitment and can help you quickly become an integral part of the team.

Moreover, seizing opportunities fosters a sense of ownership and accountability in your professional life. By actively engaging in available opportunities, you take control of your career trajectory rather than passively waiting for success to come to you. This proactive approach can lead to greater job satisfaction and a more fulfilling career. Additionally, embracing new challenges and responsibilities helps you build a diverse skill set, making you more adaptable and resilient in the face of change.

Networking is another important aspect of seizing opportunities. By volunteering for internal projects or participating in company events, you can connect with colleagues and leaders across different departments, expanding your professional network. These connections can open doors to new opportunities, provide mentorship, and offer support throughout your career.

MY STORY

Opportunity in Disguise

In 1993, I joined Western Digital as a Recruiting Coordinator, supporting the R&D Storage Division's recruiting efforts. This part-time contractor role was to fill in for someone on maternity leave. I had recently been laid off from an analyst role with a local politician in San Jose due to cost-saving measures and sought temporary employment until the job market improved, hoping to eventually return to the public sector. I had no experience in recruitment and knew very little about the disk drive industry.

Initially, I reported to Diane Karija, a senior recruiter who trained me on key recruiting processes and systems. Each day felt like my first, filled with unpredictable tasks requiring quick thinking—a challenge I found invigorating.

Over time, my responsibilities grew as Diane entrusted me with sourcing candidates and building a pipeline for hard-to-fill positions. I quickly adapted to this fast-paced environment, crucial for swift and effective hiring. This period coincided with intense competition in the disk drive industry, with Western Digital vying for top talent against major players like Seagate, Conner, Quantum, Maxtor, and IBM.

After a few months, the woman on maternity leave chose not to return, and the team offered me a full-time position. Unsure if this was my career path, I accepted the role, enjoying the work of collaborating with hiring managers, sourcing candidates, and analyzing recruitment metrics.

After about six months, a significant organizational shake-up occurred. Both Diane and another recruiter left for new opportunities, leaving the organization without any recruiters, and temporarily leaving me without a direct role. Despite these disruptions, I leveraged my familiarity with candidate schedules, hiring managers, and ongoing recruitment needs to keep things running smoothly. Although I lacked the years of experience of the senior recruiters, I was confident in my abilities and maintained momentum without missing a beat.

During this transitional period, Jim Wright, the then Director of Staffing at Western Digital, flew in from company headquarters to provide me with personal training. This one-on-one coaching focused on developing and implementing strategic sourcing strategies, gaining deeper insights into technical positions, and refining my skills in negotiating and closing senior-level candidates. Learning directly from such a seasoned industry leader significantly enriched my skills as a recruiter.

Once more, I found myself at a crossroads. Unsure of where this path would lead, I chose to seize the moment with a "can-do" mindset, motivated to embrace new opportunities. At the end of that year, the VP of Human Resources awarded me a Kudo Award for my efforts in stepping up and successfully filling multiple positions for the site. With this early success, I was officially promoted to "recruiter" during my first performance review. What began as a temporary stint in recruitment, with thoughts of returning to politics, unexpectedly blossomed into a 30-year career. Who would have imagined?

Like the stories of Tom Brady and my own experiences, every opportunity, no matter how small, is a chance to learn and grow. Approach each task with enthusiasm and a willingness to learn, and you'll discover that even the smallest opportunities can lead to significant personal and professional development.

By consistently seizing opportunities, you establish yourself within your organization as a valuable and dedicated team member, ready to take on new challenges and advance your career. As you start on your new role, cultivate confidence, seize every moment, and embrace the opportunities around you to unlock your full potential and achieve success.

RETURN TO OFFICE CHALLENGES

Let's take a moment to talk about the 'Return-to-Office' debate that many companies are grappling with at the time of writing this book. As a new hire just starting your career at your company, you may soon discover an ongoing internal battle between remote work and in-office work at your organization. Many companies are finding themselves at odds with their employees' resistance to returning to traditional office settings.

The truth is, it's not that employees don't want to return to the office again — it's that they're hesitant to return to an office experience that doesn't meet their needs[13]. If this is something you are experiencing while adjusting to your new work environment, *what can you do to ensure you are assimilating effectively as a new hire during the remote work debate?*

With no immediate return to the office in sight, creating a virtual onboarding experience that engages new hires is important. A significant percentage of employees don't want to return to the office full-time. A recent survey found that 29% of workers prefer hybrid work and 23% prefer fully remote work, meaning just over half prefer not to be fully in-office.[14] Employees are also looking for flexibility, such as four-day weeks or flex time, to better achieve the work-life balance they value.

While many employers may be flexible, not every company will be. It often depends on the industry and the specific role. There are no easy answers—what works for one organization may not work for another. My suggestion is to focus on what you can control and don't get too caught up in the broader debate.

As discussed in Chapter One, a robust onboarding experience is essential for welcoming new employees and setting them up for success. To effectively assimilate and thrive with your manager and team in a remote or hybrid setup, consider these strategies:

1. **Establish Clear Communication**: Set expectations with your manager, schedule regular check-ins, and utilize collaboration tools like Slack, Microsoft Teams, or Zoom.

2. **Stay Organized**: Use project management tools such as Trello, Asana, or Monday.com to keep track of tasks and deadlines.

3. **Be Proactive**: Initiate conversations, ask questions, and introduce yourself to colleagues to build relationships.

4. **Build Relationships**: Participate in virtual coffees, team meetings, and social events to connect with your team.

5. **Seek Regular Feedback**: Request feedback from your manager and act on it to demonstrate your commitment to growth.

6. **Maintain a Routine**: Set a daily schedule and designate a specific workspace at home to minimize distractions.

7. **Stay Visible**: Share regular updates on your progress and achievements, and ensure you are accessible during work hours.

8. **Embrace Flexibility**: Adapt to changes and maintain a healthy work-life balance. Just don't get caught up on it. This is a great opportunity to show your flexibility from your end.

9. **Continuously Learn**: Take advantage of online courses, webinars, and company-provided training programs.

10. **Show Initiative**: Take ownership of tasks and projects, and actively contribute ideas during meetings.

Making a smart, intentional effort to connect personally and professionally builds trust and respect—laying the groundwork for long-term success. By following these tips, you can effectively integrate into your team and organization, build strong relationships, and thrive in a remote or hybrid work environment—*even while the higher-ups figure out the return-to-office ordeal.*

BULLISH PRO TIPS

- **Build your own 90-day plan.** If your manager doesn't provide one, create your own with SMART goals and check-ins.

- **Say yes to stretch opportunities.** Raise your hand. Visibility and growth often come from doing what others won't.

- **Track your progress weekly.** Small wins compound. Keep a log of accomplishments, feedback, and new skills.

- **Be Tom Brady in your rookie year.** Walk in with belief, preparation, and a "no one's taking this job from me" mindset.

- **Don't overthink the office vs. remote debate.** Focus on building trust and credibility in whatever format you're given.

What you're building now—your habits, your name, your presence—lays the foundation for every opportunity that follows. Stay visible. Stay sharp. Stay bullish.

Closing Reflection:

Adapting to new ways of working takes courage. But to truly thrive, you'll need to move beyond comfort and engage with structured goals that define success.

Let's Recap!

- **Structured Onboarding:** A 90-day plan provides a clear roadmap and structure for the initial period, helping new hires effectively navigate their role and responsibilities.

- **Alignment and Expectations:** It sets expectations and goals, aligning the new hire's objectives with those of the team and organization.

- **SMART Goals:** Using SMART (Specific, Measurable, Achievable, Relevant, Time-bound) goals enables new hires to track their progress and recognize when they have achieved success.

- **Career Acceleration:** Taking proactive steps to prepare for and seize internal opportunities can significantly accelerate a new hire's career growth and successful integration into the organization.

- **Feedback and Adjustment:** Regularly reviewing progress and seeking feedback helps new hires adjust their strategies and improve performance, ensuring they stay on track to meet their goals and expectations.

Master these early days, and you won't just find your place—you'll start building your legacy.

PART ONE: SO, IT BEGINS

Key Takeaways

NOTES:_____

_____

_____

_____

_____

_____

_____

_____

ACTIONS:_____

_____

_____

_____

_____

_____

_____

_____

_____

Pause & Reflect

Before You Enter Part Two – The New World

You've made it through your first months on the job—well done. By now, you've realized that what you were taught in school only scratches the surface. The real-world workplace is fast-moving, full of unspoken rules, and driven by relationships, perception, and execution.

Take a moment to reflect:

- What were your biggest early surprises about how companies operate?

- Have you been passive—or proactive—about managing your learning curve?

- Are you documenting wins and lessons to shape your performance story?

This is just the beginning. You're about to enter unfamiliar terrain where expectations rise and growth gets uncomfortable. That's where the real opportunity is.

PART TWO

THE NEW WORLD

"Launch into work"

4

CHAPTER

———

CAREER PROGRESSION

Well done on settling into your position over the first few months! As you continue to grow in your role, it's critical that you understand and harness the power of OKRs—Objectives and Key Results. This goal-setting tool can accelerate your success in your first year of employment. Depending on the industry or company size, goal setting frameworks like OKRs—or their equivalents—may be used. OKRs are more than just goals; they are a strategic tool that aligns your efforts with the company's mission while fostering personal growth and accountability.

Step 1: Understand the Basics

As you start your new role, familiarize yourself with the OKR framework (see **Figure 4.1**). Objectives are your overarching goals—what you ultimately aim to achieve. Key Results are specific, measurable outcomes that define success in reaching those objectives. For example, your objective might be to enhance customer satisfaction, and a key result could be achieving a 20% increase in Net Promoter Score (NPS) by the end of the quarter.

OKRs	Progress	Due Date
Objective 1		
Key Result		
Key Result		
Key Result		
Key Result		
Objective 2		
Key Result		
Key Result		

Key Result		
Key Result		

Figure 4.1: OKR Template

Step 2: Align with Company Goals

Take the time to align your OKRs with your team and company's strategic priorities. This alignment ensures that your efforts contribute meaningfully to the company's success. Always discuss your OKRs with your manager for clarity and alignment.

Step 3: Set SMART OKRs

Craft SMART OKRs that are Specific, Measurable, Achievable, Relevant, and Time-bound (refer back to **Figure 3.2**). Be clear about what you want to accomplish and how you will measure your progress. For example, instead of saying "Get better at reporting," aim to "Submit three weekly dashboard reports with zero errors by the end of the quarter."

Step 4: Track Progress Regularly

Regularly monitor your progress against your key results. Use tools or simple spreadsheets to track metrics and milestones related to your OKRs. This practice keeps you focused and allows you to make adjustments if needed to stay on course toward achieving your objectives.

Step 5: Adapt and Grow

Throughout the year, be prepared to adapt your OKRs based on changing priorities or new insights. Stay flexible yet committed to your goals. Seek feedback from colleagues and managers to refine your approach and ensure alignment with evolving company needs.

Step 6: Celebrate Milestones

Celebrate your achievements along the way, whether they're big wins or small victories. Recognizing your progress not only boosts morale but also reinforces your commitment to continuous improvement and success.

By embracing OKRs early as you start your career with your company, you will establish a structured approach to your work, demonstrate initiative, and contribute effectively to your team's success. Over time, mastering OKRs will not only enhance your professional development but also position you as a proactive and valuable asset within the organization.

Let's see how one new hire, Ryanne, applied OKRs in her first months.

RYANNE'S STORY

Clarity Through Structure

Ryanne joined a software company and was eager to make a strong start. Early in her onboarding, she encountered the concept of OKRs (Objectives and Key Results), a framework designed to help employees align their goals with the company's strategic objectives. Though the concept was new to her, her manager, J.R., was ready to help her understand its significance.

During their first one-on-one meeting, J.R. sat down with Ryanne and began, "Ryanne, welcome aboard! One of the key tools we use here to ensure everyone is aligned with our company goals is the OKR framework. Let me walk you through it."

Ryanne looked intrigued but slightly apprehensive. "I've heard a bit about OKRs, but I'm not entirely sure how they work. Can you explain?"

J.R. nodded, "Of course. OKRs are essentially a way to set and track goals. They consist of two main parts: Objectives and Key Results. Your objectives are the goals you want to achieve— think of them as the destination. Key Results are the specific, measurable outcomes that indicate whether you've reached those objectives. They're like the milestones on your journey."

Ryanne listened intently, trying to grasp the new concept. "Can you give me an example?"

"Sure," J.R. responded. "Let's say one of your objectives is to improve the user experience of our software. Your Key Results might include increasing user satisfaction scores by 20% and reducing the number of support tickets related to usability issues by 30%. These Key Results give you a clear target to aim for and help measure your progress."

Ryanne nodded, beginning to see the practical application. "How do I go about setting my OKRs?"

"That's a great question," J.R. said. "Start by thinking about what you want to achieve in your role. Align those goals with the broader objectives of your team and the company. Then, set Key Results that are ambitious yet attainable. Remember, it's important that they are specific and measurable."

Ryanne smiled, feeling more confident. "I think I understand now. I'll start drafting my OKRs and come back to you for feedback?"

"Exactly," J.R. said encouragingly. "And remember, OKRs are not just a set-it-and-forget-it tool. We'll review them regularly to track your progress, make adjustments if needed, and ensure you're on the right path. It's an iterative process, and I'm here to support you throughout."

Throughout her first quarter, Ryanne embraced the OKR framework with renewed enthusiasm. She actively participated in setting her OKRs, ensuring they were both challenging and achievable. J.R.'s guidance helped her prioritize tasks that directly contributed to these objectives, streamlining her workload and clarifying her role within the team.

By the end of her first year, Ryanne had not only met but exceeded her initial OKRs, earning recognition from her team and leadership. Reflecting on her experience, she realized that embracing OKRs from day one had been instrumental in her success. J.R.'s support and the structured approach of OKRs provided clarity, motivation, and a tangible roadmap for growth within the company.

As a new hire, when you begin integrating OKRs into your professional toolkit like Ryanne did, you discover its transformative power in aligning personal aspirations with organizational goals. This structured approach accelerates your learning curve and fosters a culture of accountability and achievement across the company.

⚲AN INSIDER'S VIEW ⚲

Well-established companies rely on OKRs—Objectives and Key Results— drive strategic alignment, accountability, and performance across all levels, starting from the top level (see **Figure 4.2**).

At its core, OKRs provide a structured goal-setting framework that translates high-level strategic objectives into actionable steps, ensuring that every employee understands how their contributions directly impact the company's overarching goals.[15] They are used to align an entire team around bold, ambitious goals, while keeping them on the same page.

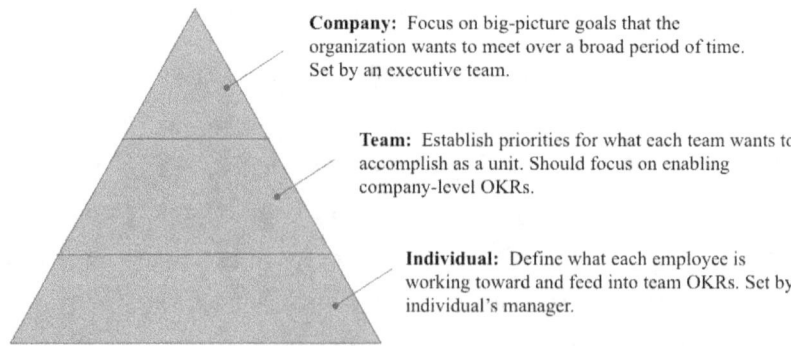

Company: Focus on big-picture goals that the organization wants to meet over a broad period of time. Set by an executive team.

Team: Establish priorities for what each team wants to accomplish as a unit. Should focus on enabling company-level OKRs.

Individual: Define what each employee is working toward and feed into team OKRs. Set by individual's manager.

Figure 4.2: Alignment of OKRs across organizational levels

OKRs provide structure and clarity to organizational priorities. By setting clear objectives that articulate what needs to be achieved, and defining measurable key results that quantify success, companies ensure that everyone is working towards the same strategic outcomes. This clarity not only aligns teams and departments but also minimizes ambiguity and enhances focus on critical initiatives.

OKRs also promote accountability within the organization. Each OKR is accompanied by specific metrics or milestones that serve as checkpoints for progress. This approach fosters a culture where employees take ownership of their objectives and are motivated to deliver results. Regular tracking and evaluation of OKRs enable teams to identify challenges early, make necessary adjustments, and maintain momentum toward achieving their goals.

Flexibility and adaptability are another key benefit of OKRs. Unlike traditional static goals, OKRs are designed to be dynamic and responsive to changing business conditions. Teams can regularly review and revise their OKRs to reflect new priorities, market shifts, or emerging opportunities. This agility ensures that the organization remains nimble and responsive in a fast-paced and competitive environment.

OKRs also drive continuous improvement within teams and individuals. By setting ambitious yet achievable goals, OKRs challenge employees to push their boundaries and strive for excellence. This focus on growth and development not only enhances individual performance but also contributes to the organization's overall capability and resilience.

OKRs foster a culture of transparency and collaboration. When objectives are openly communicated and aligned with broader company goals, it encourages cross-functional teamwork and knowledge sharing. Employees understand how their work connects to the larger mission, fostering a sense of purpose and collective achievement.

Strategically, OKRs enable companies to execute their business strategies effectively. By breaking down strategic objectives into actionable OKRs, organizations can ensure that resources are allocated efficiently, priorities are clear, and progress is measurable. This alignment of efforts across the organization enhances operational efficiency and drives sustainable growth.

As a new hire, the deeper your understanding of OKRs and their application, the greater your ability to harness their benefits. They serve as a cornerstone of effective performance management and strategic execution in most organizations. By promoting alignment, accountability, agility, and continuous improvement, OKRs empower companies to navigate complexity, drive innovation, and achieve long-term success in today's dynamic business landscape.

COMMON MISTAKES WHEN WRITING OKRs

As a new hire, facing challenges in your OKR journey is inevitable, especially when crafting them for the first time. Several common mistakes can significantly hinder their effectiveness and impact.

Here are key pitfalls to avoid:

1. **Lack of Alignment:** Setting OKRs that do not align with the company's strategic objectives or team goals can lead to misdirection and inefficiency. New hires may end up focusing on tasks that do not contribute to the organization's broader priorities.

2. **Too Many Priorities:** Overloading teams with numerous objectives can create confusion and dilute focus, making it unclear where efforts should be concentrated.

3. **Lack of Relevance:** OKRs should directly align with the new hire's role and responsibilities. Objectives that are irrelevant to their position or skill set can lead to confusion and inefficiency.

4. **Tasks Over Outcomes:** Focusing solely on completing tasks rather than achieving measurable outcomes can promote a checklist mentality instead of driving real progress.

5. **Overly Ambitious or Unrealistic Goals:** Setting OKRs that are too ambitious can demotivate new hires if goals seem unattainable. It's important to strike a balance between setting challenging objectives and ensuring they are achievable within given resources and timelines.

6. **Lack of Ambition:** Conversely, setting objectives that are too easy to achieve may lead to complacency and hinder meaningful progress.

7. **Unclear Language:** Using vague or ambiguous wording in OKRs can result in misunderstandings and misaligning efforts across teams.

8. **Neglecting Regular Review and Adjustment:** OKRs should be dynamic and adaptable. Failing to review or update them regularly as circumstances change can render them irrelevant or ineffective. Regular check-ins are essential for keeping OKRs aligned with evolving priorities.

9. **Static Goals:** Not allowing flexibility in OKRs to adapt to changing circumstances may result in pursuing outdated or irrelevant goals.

10. **Lack of Buy-In or Ownership:** Without involving new hires in the development of their OKRs or helping them understand their significance, motivation to actively pursue them may diminish. It's vital for new hires to feel ownership and accountability for their OKRs to drive meaningful progress.

To get the most from OKRs, avoid these pitfalls and stick to best practices. This includes ensuring alignment with strategic goals, maintaining clarity and realism, fostering adaptability, and embracing personal ownership. Thoughtfully written OKRs not only enhance individual performance but also strengthen the organization's ability to achieve its objectives effectively.

TRACKING WINS & PROGRESS

Throughout my career, I've worked with employees at all levels of an organization—and one key difference separates those who accelerate their growth from those who stay stuck: they track and measure their progress.

As a new hire, documenting your accomplishments, OKRs, and feedback is more than a nice-to-have—it's critical. It prevents misunderstandings, strengthens performance reviews, and helps you adjust early if you're veering off track. Managers can't always recall your wins in detail, especially if they're juggling multiple reports. Documenting your work allows for clearer, more productive conversations with your manager.

🐂 Let's Be Bullish:

Setting clear, achievable objectives gives your work purpose, clarity, and momentum. When you understand where you're going—and how to measure success—you develop ownership, accountability, and confidence in your role. This isn't just about hitting business goals; it's about growing your skills, expanding your impact, and building a career worth fighting for.

To build this discipline early in your career, use these strategies:

1. **Define Your OKRs:** Start each quarter by writing Objectives and Key Results that are specific, measurable, and tied to company goals. Clear benchmarks guide your priorities and prevent distraction.

2. **Track Your Progress:** Use a spreadsheet, project tool, or simple doc. Update it weekly. This keeps you focused, identifies problems early, and gives you a running log of

your contributions. (For example, track survey data if you're aiming to improve customer satisfaction.)

3. **Have Frequent Check-ins:** Don't wait until your review. Schedule regular 1:1s with your manager to review progress, realign priorities, and ask for feedback. These moments matter more than you think. (See Figure 4.3.)

4. **Reflect Quarterly:** At the end of each quarter, ask: What worked? What didn't? What should I double down on? Use this insight to set stronger goals next time.

5. **Stay Flexible:** Business needs shift. Be willing to pivot your OKRs when priorities change. Agility shows maturity—and ensures your goals remain relevant.

6. **Seek Out Growth:** Don't wait to be told what to learn. Join workshops. Follow industry trends. Volunteer for stretch projects. The best employees are self-directed learners.

7. **Use Feedback to Evolve:** Welcome feedback, even if it stings. Then turn it into action. This builds trust, credibility, and better performance.

8. **Celebrate Milestones:** Whether it's a big win or a quiet improvement, acknowledge it. Momentum matters—and so does taking pride in your progress.

By making this a habit early, you'll build a personal performance archive that supports promotions, salary conversations, and career growth. You'll also send a strong message to your team: you're intentional, accountable, and bullish about your future.

QUARTERLY PERFORMANCE CHECK-IN FLOW

Q4 CHECK-IN/NEW START

Teams:
- OKR Alignment for new fiscal year
Manager:
- Q4 Recap
- New Fiscal Year OKR Setting
- End-of-Year Self-Reflections

Q1 CHECK-IN

Quarterly Check-ins:
- Teams: OKRs Review & Calibrate
Manager:
- Q1 Recap & Progress
- Areas of Development
- Record & Track

Q2 CHECK-IN

Quarterly Check-ins:
- Teams: OKRs Review & Calibrate
Manager:
- Q2 Recap & Progress
- Areas of Development
- Record & Track

Q3 CHECK-IN

Quarterly Check-ins:
- Teams: OKRs Review & Calibrate
Manager:
- Q3 Recap & Progress
- Areas of Development
- Record & Track

January — April — July — October

Figure 4.3: Performance Conversation Check-Ins Timeline

Why documenting your progress is so important

Over the years, managers have often approached me as their Human Resource Business Partner to express concerns that a team member is not meeting expectations. Most times, these managers lack the documentation to support their claims. One crucial piece of advice for employees, especially new hires, is that documenting progress is essential for continued success. It can prevent misunderstandings with their manager and ensure a smooth integration into the team. By maintaining detailed records of their achievements and challenges, you offer a transparent view of your work, which helps build trust and clarity in your professional relationships.

A major benefit of documenting progress is creating a concrete record of tasks completed, milestones reached, and objectives pursued. This record is invaluable during performance reviews or regular check-ins, as it allows the new hire and the manager to refer to specific examples and data. Doing so reduces the risk of miscommunication and ensures a shared understanding of your contributions and areas for improvement.

In addition, thorough documentation helps you track your development and align with their manager's expectations. By regularly updating their progress, you can catch discrepancies early and make timely adjustments. This proactive approach keeps you on the right path and reinforces your alignment with team and company goals.

Documenting your progress also leads to more productive and focused one-on-one conversations. Presenting specific accomplishments and challenges allows your manager to provide more relevant feedback and support—rather than relying on memory or vague summaries. This level of preparation strengthens the quality of communication and demonstrates your commitment to your role and your growth.

Ultimately, documenting progress is a powerful habit for new hires—and a common thread among those who thrive early in their careers. It encourages transparency, improves communication, and helps ensure alignment on goals and expectations. By adopting this practice, you'll lay the groundwork for your professional success and contribute more effectively to your team.

BULLISH PRO TIPS

- **Learn the OKR language.** Understand how your company sets goals and align your work to those outcomes.

- **Draft your own OKRs.** Don't wait for your manager—propose objectives that show initiative and strategic thinking.

- **Track your wins.** Keep a quarterly performance doc that ties your work to measurable business impact.

- **Clarify expectations.** During 1:1s, ask: "How will success in my role be measured this quarter?"

- **Adjust when needed.** Be open to revisiting your goals if priorities shift—agility is part of being bullish.

Closing Reflection

Knowing how goals cascade through the company is only half the story. To grow, you must also embrace feedback—the honest mirror of your performance.

Let's Recap!

- **Focus and Alignment:** Goals help teams across the company find focus, align their efforts, and stay motivated.

- **Effective Framework:** OKRs provide a comprehensive framework for involving everyone in both top-down and bottom-up approaches, facilitating shared business success.

- **Regular Review:** OKRs should be reviewed quarterly and evaluated frequently to ensure alignment and progress.

- **Career Development:** Tracking achievements helps new hires set meaningful goals, plan their career development, and identify both strengths and areas for improvement.

- **Boost Confidence and Motivation:** Reviewing past achievements can enhance confidence and motivation, reinforcing belief in one's abilities and encouraging proactive engagement with new challenges.

- **Proactive Ownership:** Taking charge of your OKRs reinforces a bullish mindset—one where you shape your own growth, visibility, and future opportunities.

Mastering OKRs early in your career isn't just about hitting goals—it's about building the foundation of a career driven by purpose, visibility, and growth. That's what being bullish is all about.

5

CHAPTER

FEEDBACK MATTERS

Starting a new job is an exciting yet challenging experience, filled with opportunities for growth and development. One of the most important aspects of this early phase is engaging in performance conversations with your manager. Traditionally, many companies conduct these discussions through a process known as 'Performance Management,' which differs from an initial 90-day plan discussion with your manager.

A performance management cycle is a structured process used by organizations to evaluate and assess employee performance over a specific period. This is also the third stage, "Performance & Development," of the Employee Lifecycle (see **Figure 1.2**). During this stage, your company aims to help you develop your skills so that you improve in your role. They also want you to have a clear understanding of your scope and level of responsibilities.

Depending on when you begin your employment with the company, a performance review process typically follows a structured cycle that plays a crucial role in organizational development. This cycle serves as a framework for fostering accountability, encouraging continuous improvement, and aligning individual performance with organizational goals and priorities.

For instance, if you started your job in August shortly after graduation, the company's performance management process might commence the following March. This timeline provides you with approximately eight months of what I refer to as a "performance period" for your manager to assess your initial contributions as part of your formal review.

Given the diverse array of HR policies, tools, and techniques involved, it's important to recognize that no two performance management programs are the same across companies. Some utilize grading systems, others employ question-and-response formats, and still others emphasize a more flexible, free-form approach. Just as your company culture shapes its unique identity, your performance management system will reflect your organization's values and philosophy.

Your performance management cycle might be quarterly, annual, or continuous, depending on organizational needs, industry norms, and cultural preferences, each approach carrying its own advantages and drawbacks. These variations underscore the adaptability and tailored nature of performance management strategies in meeting specific business objectives and fostering employee development.

In the last decade much have been written about how modern companies have increasingly embraced more frequent and dynamic approaches to performance management.[16] Performance reviews are more than check-ins—they shape your trajectory inside the organization. These shifts reflect a broader trend toward agility and responsiveness in organizational management, where performance discussions serve not only to assess past achievements but also to drive ongoing growth and development.

Managers who see your growth potential don't just give feedback to fix—they give it to prepare you for what's next. Sometimes, that 'next' might be a new role in a different department or group.

Despite the differing opinions on what makes an effective performance management process, many business leaders today still express their disdain for performance reviews. They often compare the task to doing taxes—necessary, but far from enjoyable. While they acknowledge the importance of performance reviews, the process remains one of the least favored aspects of managing people. Why? Because they are often seen as awkward, contrived, and a significant waste of time.

THERESA'S STORY

When Feedback Falls Flat

Theresa, a highly successful software trainer at a cloud-based software company, had built an impressive five-year performance record. She was celebrated as the highest-rated instructor on her sales enablement team and had earned the unwavering confidence of her former manager. Her annual appraisals were informal, collegial affairs that lasted less than 30 minutes, reflecting her consistent excellence and strong reputation.

However, the departure of her long-time manager marked the beginning of a challenging transition. When a new performance planning and review system was introduced, Theresa experienced minimal interaction from AJ, her new manager. Although she received no negative feedback, the absence of communication led her to believe that a one-on-one meeting to review her self-reflections was unnecessary.

On the day of her appraisal, Theresa entered AJ's office with confidence, having diligently completed her self-reflections and performance goals. The meeting began with pleasantries.

"Good morning, Theresa. I hope you're doing well today," AJ greeted her, barely making eye contact.

"Good morning," Theresa replied, feeling a bit uneasy but optimistic about the review.

AJ handed her the completed appraisal document. "I've reviewed your performance over the past year. I'll go over my assessments, and then we can discuss any questions you might have."

Theresa nodded, ready to engage in a constructive conversation. However, as AJ started reading, the process was starkly different from what she was used to.

"Your performance has been satisfactory," AJ said, reading from the document. "However, there were a couple of incidents that raised concerns. For example, there were reports of poor course organization and delivery from a few trainees. This has been noted as an area for improvement."

Theresa's heart sank. "I wasn't aware of these specific concerns. Can we discuss how these issues were addressed or how I can better understand the feedback?"

AJ looked up briefly. "The details are in the reports. I suggest focusing on improving course organization. I've set new performance goals for you for the next year. Here's the list." He handed her a new set of objectives, barely pausing to elaborate.

Theresa glanced at the goals and then back at AJ. "I also included some development goals and self-reflections in the documents I submitted. I was hoping we could discuss those as well."

AJ barely glanced at the documents. "I didn't find those particularly relevant. The focus should be on the immediate areas that need improvement. I've also recommended a three percent raise for you, which is in line with your current performance rating."

As the meeting concluded, AJ added, "Do you have any questions or comments?"

Theresa, still in shock, managed to say, "No, I don't have any questions right now."

She quietly exited the office, her mind reeling from the unexpected turn of events. This experience marked a stark contrast to her previous evaluations and left her grappling with uncertainty about her future within the company.

Unfortunately, Theresa's recent performance appraisal did not yield positive outcomes. It reflects a common challenge: when both the employee and manager fail to fully engage in the performance management process, the experience becomes a missed opportunity—for growth, clarity, and trust.

When I spoke with peers in my professional network about the effectiveness of performance reviews, a few consistent themes emerged from both sides of the table:

TWO PERSPECTIVES: EMPLOYEES VS. MANAGERS

- **From the employee's viewpoint:** Performance conversations are far more effective when leaders come prepared, avoid last-minute cancellations, don't dominate the dialogue, and provide feedback with relevant, specific examples. Creating space for questions and open discussion makes the experience more collaborative and constructive.

- **From the manager's perspective:** A frequent challenge is resistance to feedback. Some employees react defensively or disengage altogether. This emotional friction makes performance conversations feel tense, awkward, and often unproductive.

Despite these tensions, the performance management process can absolutely be a positive experience—especially for a new hire. When done well, it creates a structured opportunity to receive feedback, understand your impact, and clarify expectations early on. Addressing minor issues before they escalate ensures that your contributions are aligned with team goals and company standards.

Performance conversations also reinforce how your role connects to the bigger picture. These check-ins foster a continuous loop of growth, trust, and learning. Frequent, high-quality feedback accelerates skill-building and increases confidence—especially in your first year, when you're still learning the ropes.[17]

If this is your first time going through a formal performance review process, don't stress—these conversations aren't about catching you off guard. Done right, they feel more like collaborative planning sessions than formal evaluations. You and your manager work together to set realistic goals, track progress, and identify what success looks like. These touchpoints help build mutual trust and make it easier to ask questions, share ideas, and talk openly about your career.

Over time, you'll see how performance conversations shape your trajectory within the company. They help establish clarity, build relationships, and define meaningful career goals. If you approach these discussions as opportunities for personal development—not just organizational assessments—you'll walk away with greater self-awareness and direction. Being actively engaged in the process now sets a foundation for future success.

So why do performance conversations matter so much—especially early in your career? Here are five key benefits of a well-run performance review process:

1. **Aligning OKRs to Business Goals:** Performance reviews provide an opportunity to ensure that every employee understands the organization's vision and goals—and how their role and OKRs contribute to overall success. This alignment enhances performance by focusing individual efforts on strategic priorities.

2. **Clarifying Job Roles:** Reviews help employees confirm their responsibilities and address any uncertainties. Clear job expectations reduce ambiguity and empower employees to take ownership of their deliverables.

3. **Regular Feedback:** Ongoing feedback strengthens communication and helps employees understand their strengths and areas for improvement. It promotes growth, boosts confidence, and increases job satisfaction by acknowledging progress and addressing developmental needs.

4. **Career Development:** Reviews offer a platform to discuss long-term goals and development paths. Setting objectives and identifying training opportunities supports both individual advancement and broader succession planning.

5. **Recognition and Rewards:** Performance management systems often include mechanisms to reward exceptional performance—whether through bonuses, time off, or promotions. Recognition boosts morale and encourages employees to consistently strive for excellence.

Performance reviews, when done right, are more than a task—they're a motivational tool. They help align individual goals with company strategy, reinforce accountability, and foster a culture of learning, achievement, and growth.

❧ AN INSIDER'S VIEW ☙

So, what's the impact of not conducting Performance Reviews effectively?

An integral performance management process involves many aspects such as goal setting, check-ins, self-reflections, and performance review. *So why is it such a big deal?* I remember a new hire asking me this question during a performance management training session I was conducting. It made me pause and think, "That's a great question." I'm certain that if I gathered all the managers in the company and announced we were no longer required to conduct performance reviews, there would be loud cheers and applause from everyone.

MY STORY

Ignored Signals, Lost Talent

Early in my career, I took on the role of VP of Human Resources for a startup CRM software company. Reporting directly to the CEO, I quickly discovered that he had strong opinions about company culture, especially regarding performance management. My CEO was adamantly opposed to implementing a performance management process, believing it would create an administrative burden and consume valuable time better spent on growing the business and generating revenue. In his previous company, my CEO saw performance reviews as primarily a way to document and manage out bottom performers rather than a tool for developing and retaining top talent.

At this company, we experienced hyper-growth following a round of funding and were hiring aggressively. However, over time, we noticed a troubling trend: many of our recent hires were resigning and leaving for other opportunities. This added significant stress to our recruitment team, as we were increasingly filling replacement positions instead of focusing on adding new roles to our overall headcount.

To understand the reasons behind this turnover, I reviewed exit interview data for employees who resigned voluntarily within their first six and twelve months of employment. The top five reasons cited for leaving were:

- Job dissatisfaction
- Lack of career growth
- Lack of training and development

- Management dissatisfaction
- Better opportunities elsewhere

These insights highlighted critical areas where we needed to improve to retain talent and support our rapid expansion.

One such instance involved a technical writer who resigned a few months after he started. Before leaving, he requested a meeting with me. He shared that during his short tenure, his manager never mentioned any formal assessment process or provided feedback on his work. His manager ignored his requests for guidance on advancing within the company.

"What I was really looking for was feedback on how I can improve and establish myself within the organization," he said. "At the end of it, there was no mention of next steps. I was very much in the dark."

Unfortunately, this story is an all-too-common example of the problems caused by an ineffective performance review process. Now more than ever, employees want to know where they stand and how to advance their careers, but most companies fail to provide that information effectively. Waiting for employees to leave without addressing their concerns is a shortsighted and ineffective approach.

In contrast, proactive performance management not only identifies opportunities for early intervention with potential issues and problematic employees but also fosters a culture of continuous improvement. As mentioned earlier, regular feedback, open communication, and development opportunities empower employees to perform at their best. By embracing this forward-thinking approach, companies will enhance individual and team performance and drive long-term success and competitiveness for the organization.

🐂 Let's Be Bullish:

As a new hire, it's never too soon to seek feedback to ensure you're on track and continuously improving in your role. Think of this as an extension of your initial 90-day plan when you initially started. To get into the habit of regularly receiving feedback, make a mental note to manage this process for yourself on a quarterly basis. Research shows that 75% of employees who receive at least monthly recognition are satisfied with their jobs.[18] These check-ins with your manager can serve as valuable opportunities to discuss your accomplishments, provide context for unmet goals, and gain insights for your priorities and/or goals for the next quarter.

You should also be prepared to share your perspective regarding your performance, what you think is going well and where you feel you could make improvements. Be sure you include successes that you are proud of, barriers that you are facing, and challenges you've encountered.

SELF-REFLECTION PROMPTS

- What challenging assignment, interaction, etc. do you feel you handled really well? What new skills did you get to practice or what strengths did you depend on to do so?

- How did you show up to support others on your team or externally?

- In what ways are you recognizing improvements in your skills or work product?

- Were there challenges that prevented you from accomplishing what you had hoped for?

- Was your manager available when you needed them?

- Do you have the tools and resources to do what is being asked of you?

In my experience, employees often struggle with writing their self-reflections, which is typically the initial phase of the performance review process. This can be a daunting task, especially when trying to recall accomplishments and areas for improvement over an extended period. To make this process easier and more effective, I strongly recommend consistently tracking your progress throughout the performance period, whether it's annually, semiannually, or quarterly.

One practical method is to start a "Ta-Da" list in a simple document. In this list, regularly record all your achievements and moments of pride throughout the year. Include praises from team members or colleagues, captured via Slack, email, or any other communication platform. Actively acknowledge all your accomplishments, even the small ones. Documenting these accolades as they happen ensures that you don't overlook or forget the small and big wins that occur over the span of 6-12 months.

This habit not only simplifies the self-reflection process but also provides a comprehensive overview of your contributions and growth. When it comes time to write your self-reflection, you'll have a detailed record of your successes and positive feedback, which makes it easier to present a well-rounded and accurate self-assessment of your performance. This proactive approach to tracking progress can boost your confidence and provide clear evidence of your impact and value to the organization.

BULLISH PRO TIPS

- **Ask for feedback early and often.** Don't wait until your formal review—create a habit of asking, "What can I do better?"

- **Keep a "Ta-Da" file.** Document praise, wins, and improvements—you'll thank yourself during review season.

- **Treat feedback like a gift, not a threat.** Even if it stings, use it to fuel your growth, not your self-doubt.

- **Write your self-reflection quarterly.** Don't scramble to remember everything—check in with yourself regularly.

- **Make performance reviews work for you.** Come prepared. Share your wins, lessons learned, and your plan to grow.

Closing Reflection

Feedback can sting, but it's the key to progress. What you do with it sets the stage for own development.

Let's Recap!

- **Understand Responsibilities and Expectations:** Performance reviews help new hires grasp their responsibilities and the company's expectations.

- **Clarify Job Roles:** Performance reviews provide an opportunity to confirm your role expectations, address any confusion about responsibilities, and ensure alignment with your manager's understanding of your contributions.

- **Receive Timely Feedback:** Regular reviews provide constructive feedback that is essential for professional development.

- **Foster Open Communication:** Performance reviews promote open communication, strengthening relationships and enhancing job satisfaction.

- **Guide Skill Development and Career Paths:** Reviews offer valuable guidance on skill development and potential career paths within the company.

- **Recognize Achievements:** Performance reviews acknowledge achievements, boosting morale and motivation.

- **Maintain a Detailed Record:** Keep a detailed record of your accomplishments, projects, and any positive feedback received.

- **Prepare for Reviews:** Be ready to discuss what you've learned, areas where you need support, and your plans for future improvement and development. -

6

CHAPTER

OWN YOUR GROWTH

"Look what I've accomplished in a short period of time; why didn't I get promoted?"

This common response from recent hires often follows their first performance review, usually with a sense of frustration or confusion. As an HR professional, it's important to help new hires understand that showing initial signs of performing well in their current role doesn't automatically warrant an immediate promotion.

As a new hire, you need to demonstrate not only your ability to perform your current tasks efficiently but also a comprehensive understanding of your role within the organization.

A promotion involves more than just completing assigned duties successfully. It requires showing initiative, contributing to the team's overall success, and exhibiting potential for leadership and greater responsibilities. New hires must show that they can think strategically, solve complex problems, and adapt to changing circumstances. While promotions for new hires can happen, they typically occur under exceptional circumstances. It's about proving that they can add value beyond their immediate tasks and contribute meaningfully to the company's broader goals and challenges.

In addition to strong performance, demonstrating a full understanding of one's role is critical. This means grasping how their work impacts other departments, aligns with company objectives, and contributes to overall business success. Recent graduates who are entering the new world of work should strive to go beyond their job descriptions by understanding the company's mission, vision, and values. They need to show that they can apply this knowledge in their daily tasks, making informed decisions that reflect an awareness of the broader organizational context.

Still keeping with the third stage, "Performance & Development," of the Employee Lifecycle (see **Figure 1.2**), continuous learning and professional development are key factors in positioning oneself for promotion. New hires should actively seek feedback from managers and peers to identify areas for improvement and growth. Taking on new projects or responsibilities, even if they are outside their immediate job scope, demonstrates a willingness to learn and adapt. Engaging in training programs, attending workshops, and pursuing relevant certifications can also signal a commitment to personal and professional growth, which is highly valued by employers.

Building strong relationships within the organization is essential. Networking with colleagues, participating in team activities, and collaborating across departments can help new graduates understand different perspectives and how various functions interconnect. By being a team player and showing a genuine interest in others' work, new hires can build a reputation as reliable and engaged employees. These relationships can provide support and guidance, helping new hires navigate their career path within the organization.

Excelling in your current responsibilities is necessary—but not sufficient—for promotion. New hires must be able to demonstrate their performance, full understanding of their role, and potential for greater responsibilities. By showing initiative, understanding the broader business context, engaging in continuous learning, and building strong relationships, new hires can position themselves for advancement and long-term success within the company. However, career progression isn't always a straight line - most times it's non-linear.

Here's what that looks like in practice. Many employees develop skills in various ways, and modern career paths are often non-linear. In many ways, today's careers are described as being more 'squiggly.'[19] As a new hire reviewing your initial performance with your manager, you can take several proactive steps to ensure growth and improvement. First, it's essential to reflect on the feedback provided, considering both your strengths and areas for improvement. If any part of the feedback is unclear, seek clarification from your manager to fully understand the expectations. Based on this feedback, set specific, measurable, achievable, relevant, and time-bound (SMART) goals that address areas for improvement while building on your strengths.

As a next step, you should develop a detailed action plan outlining the steps to achieve your goals. Include specific timelines and necessary resources to provide a clear path forward, this is a great opportunity to get feedback from others. Arrange regular check-ins with your manager to discuss your progress, ensuring ongoing feedback and necessary adjustments to the action plan.

Additionally, identify any skills or knowledge gaps and seek additional training or resources, such as workshops, courses, or mentorship, to address these areas. Implement feedback immediately in your daily tasks and demonstrate a willingness to improve, showing your commitment to your role and professional development.

NONLINEAR CAREERS: THE "SQUIGGLY" PATH

As you go through this career development process, you will soon find out that career progression doesn't follow a linear route; there are many twisting paths that lead to new opportunities (see **Figure 6.1**). Non-linear career paths can still be intentional—with thoughtful planning behind each step.[20]

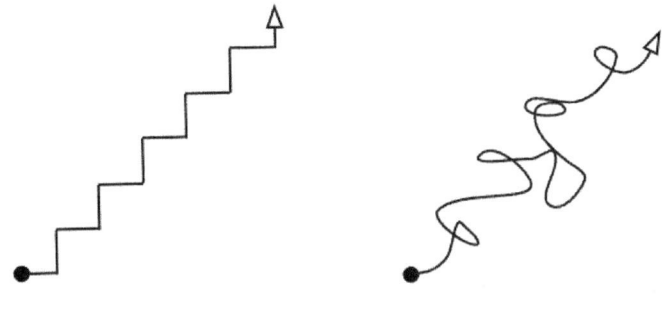

What People Think Career Path Looks Like....   What Career Path Really Looks Like....

Figure 6.1: A Career Path Liner vs. Non-Linear

Keeping your manager informed about your progress through regular updates demonstrates accountability and proactive communication. If you need support or resources, such as additional training or tools, don't hesitate to ask your manager or colleagues for help. It's important to recognize that career paths are never straightforward; they often require flexibility and adaptability.

As you begin your professional journey, learn to embrace uncertainty, and remain open to changes in direction. This flexibility can lead to unexpected opportunities and valuable experiences. Maintaining a positive attitude and viewing feedback as a chance for growth rather than criticism will help you stay focused and resilient. Treat feedback as a valuable learning tool that can guide your development and enhance your performance.

As you become more familiar with the organization, actively seek out learning opportunities and build relationships with mentors and peers who can provide guidance and support. Be willing to explore different roles and responsibilities within the organization, as this can broaden your skill set and open new pathways for advancement. Flexibility and a willingness to pivot when necessary are key to navigating a dynamic career landscape.

By taking these steps, you can effectively address feedback, demonstrate your commitment to improvement, and position yourself for future opportunities within the organization. A flexible mindset will not only help you manage the complexities of your career but also enable you to make meaningful contributions to your team and organization. Embracing the non-linear nature of career paths will ultimately lead to a more fulfilling and successful professional journey.

EMBRACING DEVELOPMENTAL OPPORTUNITIES

I'm often asked how someone can develop in their role or acquire new skills to further their growth within the company. I always welcome this conversation, not just with new hires but also with long-tenured employees. I firmly believe in nurturing talent and encouraging individuals to grow as much as possible within the organization. It is far more rewarding to see employees thrive and maximize all available opportunities rather than lose valuable talent because they haven't fully explored their potential in their current environment.

As a new hire, one of the most impactful steps you can take for your career is to actively seek out and embrace developmental opportunities. Volunteering for new projects, tasks, and responsibilities not only demonstrates your enthusiasm and commitment, but also builds essential skills and increases your visibility across the organization. By stepping out of your comfort zone and taking on challenges, you set yourself on a path toward continuous improvement and long-term career success no matter what stage of life you're at.

Taking on developmental opportunities allows you to acquire a diverse set of skills and experiences. Whether it's leading a project, participating in cross-functional teams, or learning a new software tool, each opportunity adds to your skill set and enhances your versatility. This not only makes you a more valuable asset to your current organization but also broadens your career prospects for the future. Employers value individuals who show initiative and a willingness to learn, as these traits often translate into better performance and greater contributions to the team.

As a new employee, it's essential that you begin to build a strong professional network within your organization. By collaborating with colleagues from different departments or working under the mentorship of experienced leaders, you gain insights and perspectives that extend beyond your immediate role. These relationships can provide guidance, support, and potential career advancement opportunities down the line. Showing a proactive attitude towards your development also signals to your managers and peers that you are serious about your growth, which can lead to more significant responsibilities and leadership roles over time.

Let's pause for a real story.

MY STORY

Standing Out Early

In Chapter 3, I recounted my journey when I joined Western Digital. During those initial years, I was in the early stages of my career, eagerly immersing myself in learning the company's operations and business strategies. Unlike many peers at my level, I lacked a background in Human Resources. This motivated me to demonstrate my capability in handling HR-related matters and projects while acquiring the skills needed to advance further in my career path in the new world of Human Resources.

Reflecting on those early days, I was determined to showcase my potential to upper management by seizing every opportunity to contribute to the organization. This led to them offering me a full-time position within the HR team. Now part of the HR organization, my goal was to demonstrate my value and ambition, inspired by the career trajectories of those in Director-level roles. This drive was partly fueled by my previous layoff experience, which made me determined to secure a stable career path.

The HR team at Western Digital was composed of many talented and ambitious individuals, which posed a significant challenge: *How could I stand out?* I often pondered this during my early days on the team.

Transitioning from recruitment to an HR Business Partner (formerly known as 'HR Representative'), I provided support to employees and business leaders in Western Digital's Storage Business. Under the guidance of Katherine Hansen, an experienced HR Manager, I gained valuable exposure to critical HR functions such as Employee Relations, Performance Management, Compensation and Benefits, Training and Development, HR Metrics, and Employment Law.

During this time, Western Digital pursued ISO 9001 certification, a rigorous quality management standard requiring detailed documentation and training. When executives sought volunteers to represent departments, I eagerly accepted, unaware of the full commitment involved. This role involved collaborating with a diverse team to review and streamline core business processes company wide.

This assignment proved to be a pivotal developmental opportunity, offering me invaluable insights into HR operations and contributed to Western Digital becoming the first Fortune 500 company to achieve ISO 9001 certification. Engaging in one-on-one sessions with HR leaders, business leaders, and specialists, I learned to assess and improve work processes as well as present updates to executives. We documented all HR procedures, ensuring compliance with ISO 9001 through detailed internal audits and training initiatives.

This intensive experience served as a crash course in Human Resources, particularly valuable for someone without formal HR training. It also expanded my network across functional organizations, enhancing my professional connections within the company.

As I shared my story, raising your hand for developmental opportunities instills a sense of ownership and accountability in your career journey. Leading the ISO Certification process at Western Digital's HR organization helped me gain valuable skills, knowledge, and experience that contributed to my personal and professional growth while benefiting the organization through standards compliance.

By pursuing such developmental opportunities within your company, you empower yourself to seize control of your professional development instead of passively waiting for growth opportunities to present themselves. This proactive approach fosters a growth mindset, encouraging you to continuously seek ways to improve and adapt in an ever-evolving work environment. By consistently pursuing new learning experiences, you demonstrate resilience and adaptability, qualities that are highly valued in today's dynamic business landscape.

As a new hire navigating your way through the organization, actively pursuing developmental opportunities is key to gaining new skills, broadening your professional network, and positioning yourself for future success. Embracing challenges and taking proactive steps not only enhances your individual capabilities but also strengthens your ability to contribute effectively to your organization's objectives. Remember, your career development is in your hands—don't hesitate to raise your hand and take charge of it.

THE 70-20-10 LEARNING MODEL

The 70-20-10 Model for Learning and Development is a widely recognized framework in the training profession that outlines the most effective sources of learning for successful managers.[21] According to this model (see **Figure 6.2**), individuals acquire 70% of their knowledge from job-related experiences, 20% from interactions with others, and 10% from formal educational events.

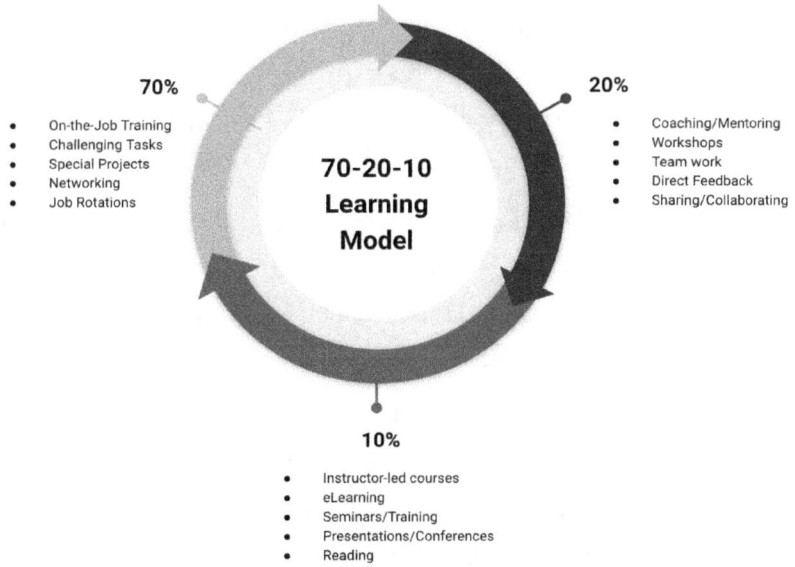

70%
- On-the-Job Training
- Challenging Tasks
- Special Projects
- Networking
- Job Rotations

70-20-10 Learning Model

20%
- Coaching/Mentoring
- Workshops
- Team work
- Direct Feedback
- Sharing/Collaborating

10%
- Instructor-led courses
- eLearning
- Seminars/Training
- Presentations/Conferences
- Reading

Figure 6.2: The 70-20-10 Learning Framework

The 70% gained from job-related experiences includes learning through challenging assignments, problem-solving, and real-world practice. These experiences allow individuals to develop skills and competencies by actively engaging in their work and tackling new challenges. As a new hire, you may notice that through experience, you are continuously gaining knowledge. This hands-on approach fosters a deeper understanding and retention of knowledge. They also learn from their mistakes and receive immediate feedback on their performance.

The 20% acquired from interactions with others involves learning through social experiences, such as coaching, mentoring, and collaboration with colleagues. These interactions provide valuable insights, feedback, and support, helping individuals to refine their skills, expand their perspectives, and enhance their professional networks. For new hires, this approach provides essential encouragement and feedback, which are crucial for their development and integration into the organization.

The remaining 10% of knowledge comes from formal educational events, including structured training programs, workshops, seminars, and courses. These events provide foundational knowledge and theoretical understanding, complementing the practical and social learning components.

By balancing these three sources of learning, the 70-20-10 Model promotes a holistic approach to professional development. It encourages new hires to seek continuous improvement through diverse learning opportunities, ultimately leading to greater effectiveness and success in their roles. This model helps new employees integrate into the organization more smoothly, fostering their growth and enhancing their contributions to the team's overall performance.

INDIVIDUAL DEVELOPMENT PLAN: WHAT IS IT?

An Individual Development Plan (IDP) is a strategic tool designed to help you drive your career, plan for growth, and take actionable steps towards your professional development. Typically created collaboratively between an employee and their manager, an IDP outlines specific career objectives, skills to be acquired, and the steps necessary to achieve these goals. Think of the IDP as a starting point that offers the freedom to reflect on your career, delve into sections that spark your interest, and think differently about your career development and future aspirations.

The IDP is not a static document but a dynamic plan that should be revisited and revised periodically to align with evolving career aspirations, job requirements, or business needs. Its primary purpose is to facilitate systematic planning and action towards achieving specific professional goals. Acting as a roadmap, the IDP guides employees in identifying the skills and competencies they need to develop in order to advance in their careers. By providing a clear vision of their career path, an IDP enhances employee motivation, job satisfaction, performance, and commitment.

As part of your individual development plan, it's beneficial to establish monthly themes of learning activities that target key areas for personal and professional growth (see **Table 6.3**). By breaking down your development goals into focused monthly themes, you create a structured approach to enhancing your skills and knowledge. Start by identifying the critical areas where you want to improve or gain expertise, such as leadership, communication, or technical skills.

Month	Theme	Focus Area
January	Leadership Skills	Engage in workshops or webinars on leadership, read books by renowned leaders, and seek mentorship from senior managers.
February	Communication	Focus on improving verbal and written communication through courses, public speaking practice, and feedback sessions.
March	Project Management	Develop skills in project management by taking online courses, managing a small project, or using project management software tools.
April	Technical Skills	Enhance your technical expertise related to your field by enrolling in relevant

		certifications or training programs.
May	Networking	Attend industry events, participate in professional organizations, and connect with peers and mentors.
June	Problem Solving	Improve these skills through case studies, puzzles, and challenging projects that require innovative solutions.
July	Time Management	Explore techniques for better time management and productivity and implement tools to help you stay organized.
August	Industry Trends	Stay updated with the latest trends in your industry by reading journals, attending conferences, and engaging with thought leaders.
September	Emotional Intelligence	Work on developing emotional intelligence through self-assessments, coaching, and

		practicing empathy in various interactions.
October	Financial Acumen	Gain a better understanding of financial principles and budgeting through relevant courses and practical exercises.
November	Strategic Thinking	Focus on strategic planning and long-term goal setting by participating in strategy workshops and scenario planning exercises.
December	Personal Reflection	Review your progress over the year, reflect on what you've learned, and set new development goals for the upcoming year.

Table 6.3: An Example of Monthly Theme Planner

For each month of your planner, select a theme that aligns with these growth areas and plan a series of activities to support it. For example, you might dedicate one month to improving your leadership skills through leadership seminars, mentorship, and reading influential books. The following month could focus on enhancing your communication skills by participating in workshops, engaging in public speaking, and practicing written communication.

Incorporate a mix of activities in your monthly theme planner such as attending relevant courses, reading industry-related materials, engaging in hands-on projects, and seeking feedback from peers and mentors. This approach not only helps in building a diverse skill set but also ensures that you are consistently progressing in different aspects of your professional development. At the end of each month, evaluate your progress, reflect on the effectiveness of the activities, and adjust your plan as needed. By maintaining this monthly focus, you will systematically develop the competencies required for your career advancement and achieve a well-rounded skill set over time.

According to a recent survey, 76% of employees indicated they would consider leaving a company if they were dissatisfied with opportunities for career progression.[22] Self-assessment and proactive career planning empower employees to envision and pursue growth opportunities, thereby enhancing employee retention. This approach fosters open dialogues between employees and managers about career aspirations and progression, cultivating a culture of continuous learning and development within the organization.

MY STORY

Rethinking Career Success

Earlier in my career, I set a personal goal that I wanted to be a Vice President of Human Resources by the age of 30, which I achieved by joining a hot software startup during the dot-com boom. Yet, despite projecting confidence outwardly, I wrestled daily with the fear of being perceived as an 'impostor" or be viewed as 'too young' due to gaps in my skill set for the HR executive leadership role. This experience reminded me that ambition without support or introspection can only take you so far. That's when I turned to my Individual Development Plan for clarity.

My CEO at this company was a visionary and passionate leader, and we had a strong relationship. However, during my tenure as a member of his executive team, while I successfully established an HR organization appropriate for the company's stage, I realized I wasn't yet operating at the level of a strategic partner he needed. This became evident as the company navigated a high-growth phase and addressed significant dysfunction within the leadership team. This marked a profound "aha" moment for me, as I realized the importance of shifting focus from my personal ambitions to making a meaningful impact on others' success.

I recall taking time to reflect on my current situation and what I needed to enhance my knowledge and skills by reviewing my IDP. This led me to a career change, moving from a traditional HR Executive path to a non-traditional role as a Leadership Development Director at a globally renowned consumer electronics company known for its innovation.

In this new role, I worked with ambitious leaders considered high potentials within the company. My responsibilities included identifying emerging leaders, designing and implementing leadership development programs, and providing executive coaching and mentorship to ensure their growth into current or future key positions.

This developmental experience provided valuable insights into industry best practices for executive talent development. I learned to create tailored development plans aligning individual career aspirations with organizational goals and became skilled in using assessment tools to evaluate leadership competencies.

I also led workshops and training sessions worldwide, focusing on essential leadership skills such as strategic thinking, effective communication, and change management. Through close collaboration with high-potential leaders, I witnessed the transformative effects of ongoing learning and development on personal and professional growth.

After several years in this role, I felt more prepared and confident to pursue my next career opportunity at a smaller yet promising company. My squiggly career journey continued with renewed focus and determination.[23]

As I shared my personal story and reflected on my non-linear career path using my IDP as a guide, I not only refined my skills in leadership development and collaborated with renowned learning and development experts but also underwent a transformative retooling process. This journey deepened my insights into how effective talent management contributes to driving organizational success.

⚲AN INSIDER'S VIEW ⚲

From a company perspective, Individual development planning (IDP) provides numerous benefits that are vital for the overall success and sustainability of the organization. Firstly, IDPs enhance employee engagement by demonstrating the organization's commitment to supporting personal growth and career aspirations. According to a recent survey, 78% of employees reported feeling more engaged and motivated when they had a clear development plan in place.[24]

Secondly, IDPs contribute to enhanced performance by aligning individual development goals with business objectives. By focusing on acquiring specific skills and competencies needed within the organization, employees become better equipped to excel in their current roles and prepare for future responsibilities. This alignment not only boosts productivity but also ensures that the company has a skilled workforce capable of meeting its strategic goals.

Moreover, IDPs play a critical role in talent retention. The same survey highlighted that 82% of employees indicated they were more likely to stay with a company that invested in their development. By investing in employees' professional growth and providing opportunities for advancement, organizations foster a culture where employees are more likely to stay long-term. This proactive approach to career development reduces turnover rates and minimizes the costs associated with hiring and training new talent.

Furthermore, IDPs support succession planning by identifying high-potential employees and preparing them for future leadership roles. This strategic approach ensures continuity in key positions and helps mitigate risks associated with leadership gaps as many companies fill key positions from internal talent with known IDPs that have specific roles identified as possible career scenarios. Additionally, IDPs promote a culture of continuous learning and innovation within the organization, as employees actively engage in ongoing skill development and knowledge acquisition.

Lastly, IDPs improve manager-employee relationships through regular discussions about career goals and progress. This open communication builds trust, enhances collaboration, and strengthens the overall workplace environment. In summary, individual development planning not only benefits employees by fostering professional growth but also contributes significantly to organizational effectiveness and long-term success.

So, what can you do today?

🐂 Let's Be Bullish:

IDP IN ACTION

Now that you've reflected on your recent performance review and explored new development opportunities, it's time to be bullish and take control of your growth—create an Individual

151

Development Plan (IDP). Thoughtful planning will help ensure that your professional growth aligns with your long-term goals.[25]

An IDP is a plan driven by you, the employee. It should detail action items, learning objectives, and the support needed to achieve specific growth goals. While it's beneficial to share your IDP with your manager for feedback, the plan should fundamentally reflect your personal career goals to ensure it resonates with you and fosters your commitment.

Here's a guide to get you started:

1. **Research Thoroughly** – Start by understanding how successful professionals in your field have advanced their careers. Leverage internal resources and seek advice from experts within your company. Expand your knowledge through industry articles, webinars, and by engaging with thought leaders and mentors. The more informed you are, the better decisions you'll make about your career development.

2. **Explore Internal Opportunities** – Have an open discussion with your manager or HR Business Partner about your career aspirations. Explore internal development programs, training, and mentorship opportunities. These resources can provide valuable skills and experiences that prepare you for future roles within the company.

3. **Identify Areas for Improvement** – Focus not just on your strengths but also on areas for growth. Assess your

skills to identify gaps and work on them. Whether it's mastering new software or enhancing public speaking, addressing weaknesses will make you a more well-rounded professional and increase your value to the company.

4. **Set SMART Goals** – Create clear and achievable objectives using the SMART framework: Specific, Measurable, Achievable, Realistic, and Timely. For example, instead of "I want to improve my public speaking," set a goal like "I will attend a public speaking workshop and deliver a presentation at the next team meeting within three months." Write down your goals and keep them visible to maintain focus and motivation.

5. **Develop a Detailed Action Plan** – Break down your goals into manageable tasks with specific deadlines. For example, if learning a new programming language is a goal, your plan might include enrolling in a course, dedicating study time weekly, and completing a project. Regularly review and adjust your plan to stay aligned with your objectives.

6. **Seek Feedback and Mentorship** – Regular feedback from colleagues, mentors, or managers can provide valuable insights and keep you on track. Mentorship offers guidance and a different perspective on your development. Don't hesitate to seek help or advice; learning from others can accelerate your growth.

7. **Celebrate Achievements** – Acknowledge and celebrate your progress, no matter how small. Reflect on what

you've learned and the distance you've traveled since you started. Celebrating achievements boosts motivation and reinforces your commitment to ongoing development.

8. **Embrace Flexibility** – Understand that career paths are often nonlinear. Be open to unexpected opportunities and adaptable to changes in your goals or the industry. Flexibility allows you to navigate your unique career journey more effectively.

As a new hire, creating a detailed IDP can be daunting. By following these steps and adopting a proactive mindset, you can strategically plan and execute a career development strategy that leads to long-term success and fulfillment in your role.

Crafting and following your IDP will enhance your career prospects and contribute positively to your organization, making your professional journey both rewarding and impactful.

And here's something most people don't realize: well-crafted IDPs don't just help you grow—they show up in talent reviews and performance discussions. These documents often influence future opportunities within your company. Leaders notice when you take your development seriously.

BULLISH PRO TIPS

Here's what career development planning looks like in practice (see **Table 6.4**):

THE DEVELOPMENT LADDER

ADVANCEMENT — Position yourself for new roles and increased responsibility

VISIBILITY — Pursue stretch assignments, learning experiences, and training opportunities

SKILLS BUILDING — Build relationships, raise your hand, and demonstrate impact across teams

FEEDBACK — Actively seek input to refine your skills and align with expectations

IDP — Set a personal development roadmap with goals, themes, and milestones

Table 6.4: Development Ladder

- **Start your IDP now.** Don't wait for your manager—map out what skills you want to build and how you'll do it.

- **Apply the 70-20-10 rule.** Learn by doing, connect with others, and invest in structured learning.

- **Volunteer for high-impact projects.** Development starts by raising your hand before you feel 100% ready.

- **Don't chase titles—chase growth.** Focus on acquiring skills that compound your value, not just quick promotions.

- **Track monthly themes.** Pick one focus area each month—communication, analytics, leadership—and build around it.

Closing Reflection:

Growth is rarely linear—and rarely handed to you. How you take charge of your career will influence how visible you become behind closed doors.

Let's Recap!

- **Pursue Developmental Opportunities:** Engaging in developmental opportunities within your company will enhance your skills, broaden your knowledge, and accelerate your professional growth.

- **Understand Nonlinear Career Paths:** A nonlinear career path, often described as a 'squiggly' career, is less predictable than a traditional linear career ladder and involves various twists and turns.

- **Intentionality in Nonlinear Paths:** While a nonlinear career path may seem unpredictable, each step is intentional and contributes to career growth in a dynamic manner.

- **Utilize an Individual Development Plan (IDP):** An IDP is a tool designed to help employees achieve their personal and professional development goals.

- **Regularly Update Your IDP:** IDPs should evolve with the employee's career, incorporating new goals and opportunities. Regular review and updates by both employees and managers ensure the plan remains effective and relevant.

PART TWO: THE NEW WORLD

Key Takeaways

NOTES:_____

_____

_____

_____

_____

_____

_____

_____

ACTIONS:_____

_____

_____

_____

_____

_____

_____

_____

_____

Pause & Reflect

Before You Enter Part Three – Earn Your Wings

You've now seen how performance is tracked, measured, and discussed behind the scenes. You've also confronted the challenge of owning your development—whether your manager is helpful or not. Growth isn't a straight line. It's often messy, nonlinear, and entirely up to you.

Take a moment to reflect:

- Have you aligned your daily work to measurable outcomes or goals?
- Are you waiting for development to happen—or steering it yourself?
- Who knows about your aspirations—and who's helping you rise?

Now comes the turning point. It's time to be seen. Not just as someone doing the job—but as someone ready for what's next.

PART THREE

EARN YOUR WINGS

"Time to spread wings"

7

CHAPTER

BEHIND CLOSED DOORS

At this point, you may have celebrated your one-year anniversary with the company and have experienced many of the aspects covered in the first six chapters of this book as you continue on your professional journey. But here's the reality: your performance is still under constant observation. From the moment you step into your role, actions, decisions, and interactions contribute to the overall perception of your capabilities and potential within the organization.

As someone who has spent three decades in Silicon Valley, I've encountered a persistent myth in corporate circles that job security is guaranteed by exemplary performance alone. This view often portrays corporations in a paternalistic light, where employees are expected to pledge lifelong loyalty, or they get too comfortable in their roles in exchange for protection. You'll often hear this reflected in statements about the company feeling like a 'family' or emphasizing a familial company culture. You'll often hear this in companies that describe themselves as a 'family.' While well-intentioned, that narrative can lead to misplaced reliance.

As mentioned in Chapter One, your new peers, colleagues, and managers are watching every move. What I mean by this is your performance —especially if your company engages in 360-degree feedback where input from many is provided as part of the overall performance management process. Dealing with coworkers who watch your every move can be a challenging and frustrating experience. The constant feeling of being scrutinized can create an uncomfortable environment for you that hampers productivity, collaboration, and workplace morale.

Keep in mind that every task you undertake, every project you handle, and every interaction you have with colleagues and customers is an opportunity to showcase your skills and professionalism. Even seemingly minor actions can leave a lasting impression. Therefore, approach each task with diligence and a commitment to excellence.

Feedback, whether formal or informal, plays an important role in your growth. Embrace feedback as a valuable tool for improvement rather than criticism. Actively seek feedback from your peers, managers, and mentors to understand how your performance aligns with expectations and where there are opportunities for enhancement.

Remember, consistency is key. Demonstrating reliability and a strong work ethic builds trust and credibility over time. Strive to meet deadlines, communicate effectively, and collaborate with others proactively. Your ability to deliver consistent results will get noticed by others and your ability to adapt to challenges will set you apart and contribute to your long-term success in the company.

Having worked with numerous high-tech companies over the years, my advice to everyone and anyone is clear: *"Never let your guard down at work."* This isn't about instilling fear or making you constantly look over your shoulder. Instead, maintain a positive attitude and a willingness to learn. Stay curious about your industry, your company culture, and the opportunities for growth that lie ahead. By staying proactive and demonstrating a commitment to your professional development, you'll not only excel in your current role but also position yourself for future opportunities within the organization.

As a Human Resources Executive, I've collaborated closely with numerous business leaders on talent management processes, including succession planning and talent calibrations. As an employee, you may not have visibility into these talent review conversations, but they do happen, often behind closed doors.

During these talent review processes, members of the organization look at a variety of factors, such as employee potential, current capabilities, and future organizational talent needs. As a recent hire, knowing this can help you make more intentional decisions in your role. Organizations often use the 9-

box framework to guide their assessment (see **Figure 7.1**). This organizational tool helps define company goals and standards while simultaneously evaluating employee performance and potential.

⌕AN INSIDER'S VIEW ⌕

The 9-box grid is an organization development tool for assessing employee performance and potential. It provides a structured framework that helps organizations strategically manage their talent pipeline. By segmenting employees based on performance and potential, organizations can make informed decisions about resource allocation, development initiatives, and succession planning. As a new employee, you might not be familiar with this process, as it typically starts with the first level of management in a bottoms-up approach.

Figure 7.1: The 9-Box Grid for Talent Management

The 9-box grid, first introduced by McKinsey & Company in the 1970s, is a widely used tool by various companies for assessing employee potential and performance.[26] Organizations around the world have adopted it, and if your company isn't using it as part of their talent calibration meetings, it's likely utilizing a variation of this tool.

The first step in using a 9-box grid is to assess an employee's performance, which is typically done by evaluating performance reviews and reviewing self-evaluations. Managers are tasked with ranking employees based on performance and behavior, and then those rankings are passed onto upper management and leaders who can then identify and rank employees for their leadership potential. Employees can rank as low, medium, or high performance depending on how well they meet the requirements of their role.

The 9-box grid framework helps organizations clarify which employees are driving success today—and who might lead tomorrow. The horizontal axis represents an employee's potential, and the vertical axis represents their current performance. The matrix is divided into three sections, each with three boxes representing high, medium, and low potential/performance.

For high-performing employees with high potential (often found in the top right quadrant of the grid), the focus is on nurturing their growth through challenging assignments, leadership development programs, and opportunities that prepare them for future leadership roles. These employees are considered as critical to the organization's long-term success, and investing in their development ensures continuity in leadership and innovation.

Employees who perform well in their current roles but show limited growth potential (typically in the middle right quadrant) are valued for their reliability and competence in executing day-to-day tasks. While they may not be targeted for immediate advancement, they play a crucial role in maintaining operational stability and can benefit from skill enhancement programs that deepen their expertise.

Conversely, employees with high potential but inconsistent performance (top left quadrant) require targeted interventions to address performance gaps while leveraging their potential for future leadership roles. As a recent graduate, you may be viewed as a 'potential gem,' as your tenure may not yet provide sufficient data to assess your performance thoroughly, which may initially place you in a favorable quadrant.

Over time, management will want to see you in the 'high potential' quadrant. For longer-tenured employees positioned in this quadrant, the next steps typically involve targeted coaching, mentoring, or skill development initiatives aimed at bridging the gap between their current performance and their expected potential.

Employees in the bottom left quadrant, characterized by low performance and low potential, pose challenges that require careful management and HR involvement. Organizations may need to assess whether these individuals are in roles that suit their skills and interests or if additional support and development can help improve their performance and potential contribution. As a recent hire, you want to avoid this quadrant and steer clear of being considered a 'bad hire'.

By using the 9-box grid, organizations gain clarity on where to focus their efforts to maximize employee potential, drive engagement, and align talent management strategies with business objectives. One of the biggest benefits of the 9-box grid is identifying the most valuable talent in the organization. Calibrating with other leaders to identify the highest performers helps inform talent retention and development strategies. Companies can get a clear picture of where and how to divert resources to further support these high potential employees.

Much time is invested in this 9–box grid review process by management teams. It's not an easy process and it can't be rushed. For employees who do not fall into the highest performance categories, the 9-box grid offers valuable insights into how to support and develop these employees. It highlights those who may benefit from additional training or mentorship and helps managers create targeted strategies to address performance issues.

For those employees identified as "at risk," the grid facilitates the development of performance improvement plans to either improve their contributions or manage their transition out of the organization (will cover more in Chapter Eight). This approach ensures talent strategies remain focused on developing those who bring the most value to the company.

Let's take a look at what this can feel like through Bryant's story.

BRYANT'S STORY

Waiting to Be Seen

Bryant is a product designer working at a software company. He came to me to discuss his future with the company. It wasn't a resignation, but he wanted to know where he stood with his management team.

"I love my team," Bryant began when he came to my office. "Leslie who is on my team, is considered a high-potential employee—she's smart and a very hard worker. I think she deserves to be recognized as a high potential employee, but at the same time, I feel terrible for being upset about not being given the same opportunities."

Bryant shared that his educational background is not in design, but he worked his way to a designer's position and applied for it seven years ago. "Leslie joined the company just last year. She knows the projects we work on very well and she has a UX design background. I accept that there is a significant deficiency in my knowledge base, and I am working hard to learn and understand the field," he continued. "I work about 10-11 hours a day, and my manager says I do a great job, especially since I'm essentially handling 1.5 times the work someone in my position should be doing."

He paused, reflecting on his journey. "It's been a steep learning curve for me, transitioning from a non-design background to this role. I've put in a lot of extra hours and effort to bridge the gap, and I've taken on additional responsibilities to prove myself. My manager acknowledges my hard work, but I still feel overlooked when it comes to high-visibility opportunities."

As I listened to Bryant, I realized that he was frustrated. "I feel so demoralized when they give Leslie opportunities to attend big meetings, network with upper management, and run workshops and meetings for the team at big division gatherings, while I am left feeling like a cog in the wheel."

I asked Bryant how I could help. "I'm not sure if I'm just being jealous—or if something deeper is going on—but it's eating at me, partly because Leslie and I are good friends," he admitted.

I could see how much this was affecting him, both professionally and personally. "Bryant," I said, "It's completely natural to feel this way. You've worked incredibly hard to get where you are, and it's important to address these feelings. Let's discuss some strategies to help you gain more visibility and recognition within the company. Perhaps we can start by identifying specific skills or areas of expertise that you can focus on developing further, and we can also look into mentorship opportunities that can provide additional support."

Bryant nodded, seeming a bit more hopeful. "Thank you. I just needed to hear that I'm not overreacting and that there's a path forward."

Sometimes, feeling overlooked doesn't mean you aren't valued—it just means you haven't been fully seen yet.

Bryant's story highlights the importance of acknowledging the emotional and professional challenges faced by employees who feel undervalued despite their hard work. It highlights the necessity for transparent communication regarding career development opportunities and the criteria for high-potential status, whether disclosed openly by the organization or managed more discreetly behind closed doors. Bryant's experience, like that of many others, emphasizes the proactive approach of seeking feedback and mentorship to align personal growth with organizational expectations.

VISIBILITY vs. VALUE

Bryant's story is a strong example of how being valuable isn't always enough if others don't see it. In many companies, perception plays a major role in career advancement decisions. You may be delivering results, but if you're not visible to decision-makers, your growth can stall. On the other hand, some employees receive high-profile opportunities due to visibility alone—not always because they're the most capable.

Figure 7.2 offers a visual framework to assess how visibility and perceived value interest inside an organization.

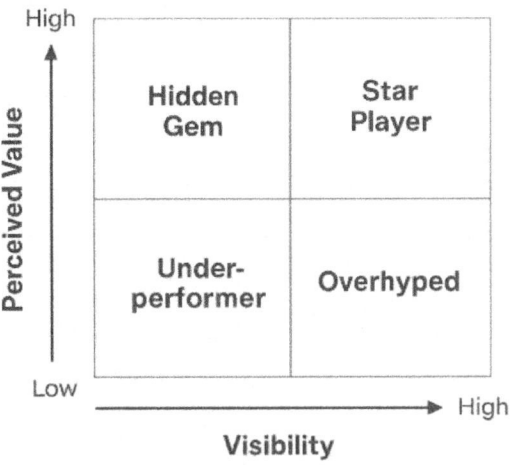

Figure 7.2: Visibility vs Value Matrix

- **Hidden Gem**: You consistently deliver strong results, but your contributions are not widely recognized. This is where Bryant likely felt he was positioned—valuable, but overlooked.

- **Star Player**: The ideal scenario. You're seen as both a high performer and a high-potential employee. These individuals are often tapped for promotions and stretch assignments.

- **Underperformer**: Neither visible nor contributing meaningfully. This often signals disengagement or a poor fit.

- **Overhyped**: These employees are highly visible but offer limited actual value. While they may gain attention temporarily, their performance rarely sustains long-term trust.

The takeaway? Don't rely on performance alone. Your goal should be to operate in the Star Player quadrant—delivering strong results and ensuring your impact is visible to the right people. This doesn't mean self-promotion for the sake of it, but rather advocating for your work, building relationships, and taking on roles that increase your exposure.

In similar scenarios, Bryant's story reinforces the critical role of clear communication and transparency in talent management. Understanding the criteria and pathways to achieving "high potential" status is essential for employees committed to advancing their careers. Organizations benefit from clearly defining these standards while ensuring equitable access to development opportunities and recognition—all while navigating the need to manage such processes discreetly.

ADVANTAGES OF A 9-BOX TALENT REVIEW

As someone who has facilitated numerous talent reviews and calibrations with business leaders, I recognize that the significance of this process lies not merely in the tool itself. The 9-box grid serves as a catalyst for discussions on succession planning and identifying emerging leaders, which is the ultimate goal. Through 9-box calibration sessions, leaders can engage in thoughtful contemplation, strategic planning, and productive discourse. This tool provides a rapid and effective way to gain insights into how leadership perceives and values individual employees, eliciting diverse perspectives and opinions when multiple leaders participate. This approach fosters a comprehensive understanding of the organization's talent pool and helps identify potential successors for key roles.

Exposes Gaps in Teams

Identifying skill and knowledge deficiencies in individuals helps business leaders understand the overall competency gaps within their teams. This insight may indicate the need for extensive training initiatives, such as broader training programs, when specific shortcomings are prevalent across multiple individuals. Additionally, it highlights the need to enhance access to professional development opportunities and foster a culture of mentorship within the organization.

Simplifies Hiring and Recruitment

Recruiting and training new team members can be expensive, especially for critical positions. Filling a vacant position with an internal candidate is a more cost-effective approach, necessitating that organizations have a firm grasp of their existing talent pool and cultivate leaders from within. Talent management tools like 9-box grids are instrumental in identifying potential internal candidates for promotion or critical roles. Those identified as 'high potential' employees may be considered for key roles across the company, ensuring that valuable institutional knowledge and experience are retained. This method not only saves costs but also boosts employee morale and loyalty by demonstrating a commitment to internal career development, leveraging the current talent pool for positions that might otherwise be filled by external candidates.

Identify Valuable Talent

The 9-box grid enables organizations to identify high-achieving individuals who exhibit significant potential to evolve into future leaders. Resources can then be allocated strategically to nurture and cultivate the next generation of leaders. When internal promotion opportunities arise, the 9-Box grid provides insights into the appropriate candidates for these positions.

Highlight Development Opportunities

Examining the 9-Box grid to identify high-potential leaders also brings attention to individuals who may not currently be well-suited for their roles or may have skill gaps. HR professionals and managers can offer tailored support to help these employees achieve their next career objectives, facilitating their development into more productive team members.

Facilitates Gathering Multiple Perspectives

Completing a 9-Box grid effectively requires data from a variety of sources, including performance evaluations, skills assessments, training records, certifications, and input from managers, peers, and HR. This comprehensive approach ensures that evaluating an employee goes beyond the intuition or subjective judgment of a single manager or leader. It reduces the likelihood of overlooking critical skills, capabilities, or weaknesses, as multiple parties are involved in the assessment process.

Creates Consistency in the Performance Process

Many organizations use the 9-Box grid to harmonize the perspectives of senior leadership and mid-level managers during performance reviews. Leadership and management teams must reach a consensus on performance standards and align on what is expected of top performers for this tool to be useful. They must collectively establish clear definitions for high, medium, and low performance. This process enhances the precision of leaders' expectations and objectives for the organization.

DISADVANTAGES OF A 9-BOX TALENT REVIEW

While the 9-Box is widely used for assessing employee potential and planning succession, it comes with significant drawbacks that can impact organizational effectiveness. From susceptibility to manager bias and the challenge of distinguishing between performance and potential, to its limited reliability in predicting future success, the 9-Box grid poses several challenges. These issues can hinder accurate talent management decisions, potentially leading to misidentified high-potential individuals, reduced diversity efforts, and employee dissatisfaction. It's critical for organizations to navigate these pitfalls carefully to optimize their talent management strategies.

Subject to Manager Bias and Misunderstanding

Despite incorporating data from various sources, it can be challenging to separate personal bias from employee evaluations. Personality traits, communication breakdowns, and individual inclinations can affect a manager's impartiality. Leaders must be aware of their predispositions and recognize that no tool is perfect.

Lacks Reliability

There isn't any universally accepted or highly reliable method for assessing individual potential for succession planning. A 2015 study found that companies predicting whether an employee would advance two levels within five years were correct only 52% of the time. This limited predictive accuracy suggests that organizations often misidentify or overlook potential future leaders.

Scarcity of Objective Measurement Data

The 9-Box framework is effective only with reliable data. Comparing individuals is challenging without consistent assessment data to evaluate performance and competencies. HR professionals often struggle to measure potential, resilience, motivation, and performance accurately. Regular reassessment of competencies and future demands is essential, and different roles may require varied assessment approaches.

Distinguishing Between Performance and Potential

Performance and potential can be difficult to distinguish without precise definitions. While performance assessments are typically established, evaluating potential is less familiar, leading to inaccuracies. Without well-defined processes, performance evaluations are susceptible to unconscious biases.

Risk of "Boxing In" Employees

Categorizing employees into the nine boxes can create a perception of fixed classification. This approach risks job stagnation and frustration, as employees may feel pigeonholed instead of being seen as having growth potential.

Impact on Historically Marginalized Employees

The subjectivity of the 9-Box tool can negatively affect historically marginalized employees. Unconscious biases may result in these individuals receiving lower rankings and being overlooked for leadership positions. A recent study, the report found that women received lower "potential" ratings than men despite higher job performance ratings, hindering DEI efforts and reducing overall diversity as these employees seek opportunities elsewhere.[27]

Employee Reactions

While transparency in sharing performance data can enhance accountability, it also carries risks. Employees receiving lower ratings may feel demotivated, and openly revealing quadrant placements can disrupt team dynamics by creating hierarchies among potential successors. Consequently, not all employees are privy to these discussions unless directly involved, typically through their managers. Often, these evaluations occur behind closed doors, limiting transparency.

Stressful Process

Determining an individual's category can be emotionally charged and subjective, often leading to stressful discussions. In my experience facilitating these talent calibration meetings,

177

disagreements over how employees are perceived can escalate into heated arguments during these sessions. Establishing a shared vocabulary and clear assessment standards is critical to fostering constructive discussions. Supporting opinions with concrete data and involving third-party HR Business Partners can significantly mitigate these challenges, ensuring fair and objective evaluations.

Unlocking a Better Performance Management Process

As a new employee entering the workforce, it's important to understand that every tool, including the 9-box grid, comes with its own set of strengths and weaknesses. Each organization operates uniquely, so what proves effective in one setting may not necessarily work well in another. Despite its alignment with overall talent management strategies, companies should approach the 9-Box grid cautiously. Addressing inherent biases among managers and potential employee concerns is crucial to leveraging this tool effectively.

🐃 Let's Be Bullish:

ARE YOU A HIGH POTENTIAL?

A survey reveals that 75% to 90% of individuals believe they excel in positive personality traits and performance.[28] This overconfidence often spans various domains such as intelligence, collaboration, and job effectiveness. Gaining an understanding of talent management processes and their significance can empower you to proactively steer your career development. However, many organizations do not openly disclose their criteria for identifying high-potential employees, making it challenging to gauge your standing or how you are perceived.

Aspiring early in your professional career to be recognized as a "high potential" within your organization is an ambitious goal. Achieving such recognition can yield substantial career benefits, such as involvement in strategic initiatives, priority for promotions, access to senior-level mentoring, and participation in leadership development programs.

To enhance your prospects of being acknowledged as a high-potential employee, it's essential to look beyond performance reviews and actively seek out your organization's criteria for identifying future leaders. One effective approach is to consult with your HR Business Partner or a Learning & Development specialist, who can provide valuable insights into what it takes to stand out and advance.

Understanding these criteria enables you to strategically cultivate the skills and qualities most valued for career progression. Focus on areas such as targeted training, tackling challenging projects, or seeking mentorship from senior leaders. This proactive stance not only boosts your visibility but also demonstrates your dedication to contributing significantly to the organization's success. Aligning your growth with the company's expectations ensures you are well-positioned to assume leadership roles and drive your career forward effectively.

To meet and exceed the high expectations associated with being a high-potential employee, consistently demonstrate exceptional performance and initiative. This involves not only fulfilling your core responsibilities with excellence but also seeking opportunities to innovate and add value beyond your immediate role. Volunteer for cross-functional projects or committees, as these experiences can showcase your ability to collaborate across teams and influence broader organizational outcomes. Additionally, regularly solicit feedback from peers and supervisors to identify areas for improvement and act on them swiftly. This shows a commitment to continuous improvement and a willingness to adapt, both of which are key traits of high-potential employees.

Building strong relationships with key stakeholders and decision-makers within your organization is also crucial. Cultivate a network of influential contacts and seek out opportunities to engage with senior leaders. By positioning yourself as a reliable and knowledgeable contributor, you enhance your visibility and reinforce your readiness for more significant responsibilities. Finally, stay informed about industry trends and organizational changes, as this knowledge enables you to anticipate and respond to evolving business needs effectively.

BULLISH PRO TIPS

- **You're always being evaluated.** From your first project to hallway interactions, your reputation is forming—own it.

- **Understand the 9-box grid.** Learn how companies evaluate performance vs. potential—it shapes your trajectory.

- **Ask how you're perceived.** Don't just assume—you can say, "How do others see me? Where do I stand today?"
- **Visibility matters.** Raise your hand for cross-functional projects and leadership moments. Be seen.
- **Aim for high potential—but earn it.** Performance opens the door; leadership behavior gets you promoted.

And here's the thing—

The 9-box grid doesn't just shape performance conversations—it also influences who gets tapped for stretch assignments or internal moves. If you've ever wondered how some employees "suddenly" land cool new roles, this is often where it begins.

Closing Reflection:

Decisions about your future often happen when you're not in the room — or even unaware. And just as quickly, external changes like reorganizations can shift your path overnight.

Let's Recap!

- **Comprehend the 9-Box Grid:** The 9-box grid evaluates employees based on current performance and future potential, aiding in talent management and succession planning.

- **Leverage Your Position on the Grid:** Understanding your position on the 9-box grid, if communicated by your manager, can highlight areas for improvement and guide your focus on developing key skills and competencies.

- **Seek Regular Feedback:** Actively seek feedback from your manager to understand your standing on the 9-box grid. Use this insight to set clear, achievable goals aligned with the organization's expectations.

- **Stay Proactive and Engaged:** Continuously seek new challenges, participate in training programs, and demonstrate your potential through consistent performance and a readiness to take on leadership roles.

Remember: growth isn't just about being great at your job—it's about being seen for it, too.

8

CHAPTER

CHANGE IS COMING

O ne day, you're confidently contributing at work, and the next, you're reading an email titled something like "Organization Updates" or attending an All-Hands meeting where the executive team talks vaguely about "strategic priorities" and "alignment." What's not being said? You've just been reorg'd.

Reorganizations are rarely introduced with full transparency. You might hear that teams are "realigning," roles are being "clarified," or leadership is "transitioning." In reality, your team may be dissolved, your manager replaced, and your reporting lines completely restructured. Whether you're personally impacted or not, this kind of organizational change triggers stress, uncertainty, and discomfort.

I've seen it all—cost-cutting initiatives, executive shakeups, product team restructures, and even full department closures. As an HR leader with three decades of experience, I've sat in the rooms where these decisions are made. I've had to deliver the news, support the aftermath, and yes, I've also been on the receiving end. These moments are never easy. They shake your confidence and challenge your sense of stability. But I want you to hear this loud and clear: **you are not alone** and unfortunately this is more normal than you might think.

WHAT TO EXPECT WHEN YOU'RE REORG'D

Change of this magnitude can feel chaotic. And here's the truth: that chaos doesn't always mean the reorg is failing. In fact, *a certain amount of disorder is expected*. Meetings will feel disjointed. Leaders may not have clear answers. Priorities shift overnight. Projects get paused or outright canceled.

You might bounce between teams or managers before anything stabilizes. And yes, roles may disappear. Even if you keep your job, the uncertainty can leave you feeling adrift. This is especially hard if it's your *first* reorg. You'll have questions—and get very few answers.

That's because reorgs are often reactions to systemic problems: missed business targets, poor product-market fit, high attrition, unsustainable burn rates, or leadership missteps. You probably won't be told this outright, and that's by design. As uncomfortable as the ambiguity feels, it protects people's dignity and keeps internal performance issues private.

Be on the lookout for vague terms like "resource optimization," "rightsizing," or "strategic focus." These are often early signs of upcoming layoffs. Don't panic—but **start paying attention**.

You might hear "this will be good for your development" or "we're excited about what's next," but inside you feel disoriented. That disconnect is real. It's not you. It's the moment. The corporate engine wants to heal quickly and move on. But as employees, we're still processing.

ISABELLA'S STORY

When Everything Changed

Isabella joined her company right after graduation and, within two years, had built a solid reputation as a rising product analyst. She consistently hit her performance targets, led cross-functional projects, and had just been invited to present in front of senior leadership. Things were going well—or so she thought.

Then came the email: **Subject: Strategic Realignment Announcement**
An all-hands meeting was scheduled for the next day.

At the meeting, leadership shared a slide deck filled with buzzwords: *efficiency, streamlined operations, new business priorities.* But the message was clear—teams were being restructured, and roles would shift. Isabella's manager was suddenly gone. Her team was split up. She now reported to a director she had never worked with, supporting a product she had zero experience with.

"I felt like the floor dropped out from under me," Isabella later shared. "No one explained anything. It was just, 'Here's your new team and your new priorities—let's move forward.'"

She tried to make sense of it.

"Why was my manager let go?" she asked her new lead.

"I can't speak to that," he replied, keeping his tone neutral.

"Is our product still a priority?"

"It's part of the new vision, yes."

That was the only explanation she received.

HR hosted a follow-up meeting and introduced the Employee Assistance Program (EAP). One of the HR reps said, "We understand this is a difficult time, and we're here to support you. Please don't hesitate to reach out." But to Isabella, it felt hollow.

"It was like they ripped off a Band-Aid where it still hurt," she said. "Then handed us a box of tissues and expected us to be fine the next day."

At first, she felt completely invisible. Meetings went on without her input. Workstreams she previously led were reassigned. Even her calendar looked empty. But after a week of waiting and wondering, Isabella decided to stop being passive.

She scheduled one-on-ones with the new team leads and, in each, asked a simple question:

:"How can I be helpful in this new setup?"

Some didn't have a clear answer. Others appreciated her initiative. Slowly, she began carving out a role for herself again.

She also started documenting everything she was learning—who the new decision-makers were, how priorities had shifted, and where she could plug in value. She reached out to a senior colleague who had survived a past reorg and asked, "How did you stay grounded when everything around you changed?" That conversation turned into an informal mentorship.

Three months later, Isabella wasn't just surviving—she was thriving. She had built credibility with her new director, secured a seat on a cross-functional strategy group, and even gained a sponsor in the product leadership team.

"It was the hardest chapter of my short career so far," she told me. "But it taught me something important—things can change fast, even when you're doing everything right. But I can change, too. And I did.

Isabella's story is just one example of how quickly the ground can shift beneath your feet. But what many employees never see is what's happening on the other side of the curtain. Behind every reorg is a flurry of meetings, decisions, and emotional weight carried by leadership and HR. So let's pull back the curtain and talk about what really goes on behind the scenes when companies decide to change course.

AN INSIDER'S VIEW

WHAT REALLY HAPPENS

Here's the part no one talks about: reorgs don't happen overnight. And they're never as clean or calm behind the scenes as they may seem on the surface.

When layoffs or major shifts are in play, HR teams go into overdrive. I've led, contributed to, or participated in these efforts—and I'll be honest—it's one of the hardest things HR professionals do. We're juggling spreadsheets, meetings across time zones, legal reviews, budget constraints, and most importantly: people's livelihoods.

We build detailed timelines two to three weeks in advance, all while trying to maintain confidentiality and carry on as if it's business as usual. We plan everything down to the hour—who's impacted, who delivers the message, how payroll and benefits will transition, what severance looks like, and how we communicate internally and externally. In the final days leading up to the announcement, we meet daily. It's not careless. It's orchestrated.

Still, no matter how polished the plan, it never feels good. Managers and HR professionals carry the emotional weight. We answer the same question 50 times as if it's the first. We support managers who may disagree with decisions. We absorb the fear, confusion, and sometimes anger. And through it all, we do our best to preserve people's dignity.

The hardest truth? HR doesn't decide who goes. That's determined by leadership. But we do influence how it feels—and we often push back and ask hard questions about why someone was selected. Our job is to make the experience as "least awful" as possible. Empathy without pity. Clarity without cruelty. We want those exiting to feel that their contributions mattered, and those remaining to still believe in the company's future.

And here's another truth: layoffs are rarely about individual performance. Often, companies hire based on aggressive projections—planning for growth that never materializes. A workforce built for 50% growth becomes excessive when reality dips to 20%.

Sometimes, a strategic pivot renders even high-performing teams redundant if their work no longer aligns with the company's direction. And yes, occasionally, companies use layoffs to remove problematic employees they couldn't exit otherwise due to lack of documentation.

If this is your first reorg, you likely won't get the full story. But now you know: it's not always about you or your performance. It's about numbers, forecasts, business models, and shareholder expectations. It's not personal—but it is painful.

When everything feels unstable, don't freeze. Use the 4P's framework to reset your mindset and act with intention.

4P's	Action	Why It Matters
Pause	Take a breath. Avoid knee-jerk reactions or gossip.	Keeps your reputation intact.

Probe	Ask thoughtful questions about your team, priorities, role.	Helps reduce ambiguity and shows maturity.
Position	Realign your strengths to the new org structure.	Makes you visible and value.
Plan	Assess your options, stay, explore internal moves or exit.	Gives you time to plan and direction.

Table 8.1: The "4P's" to Handle Change

🐂 Let's Be Bullish:

If you're still with the company after a reorg, that's worth recognizing. While these decisions are rarely personal, the fact that you remain suggests that leadership sees potential in you—and that your role, skills, and work ethic are aligned with the organization's future direction. That's a vote of confidence, even if unspoken. That doesn't mean you're immune from future changes—but it does mean you're in a position to contribute, grow, and help shape what comes next.

Reorgs are rarely graceful. They test your patience, emotional maturity, and professional resilience. But as you saw with Isabella, staying curious, proactive, and grounded can help you emerge stronger.

Loyalty feels great when times are good. But companies don't operate on loyalty—they operate on profitability and survival. Be bullish about your career. Build relationships, do great work, but never forget: you are your own best advocate.

Don't get swept up in hallway gossip or sink into disengagement. Focus on what you *can* control: your attitude, your output, your learning (see **Table 8.1**). If you keep chopping wood and carrying water, others will take notice.

Remember: being bullish isn't about being fearless—it's about showing up, even when the future feels foggy.

BULLISH PRO TIPS

- Pay attention to company earnings calls and internal memos.
- Watch for hiring freezes, travel budget cuts, and leadership departures.
- Keep your resume updated—even if you're not looking.
- Document your wins and impact every quarter.
- Loyalty is admirable. But preparedness is power.

Closing Reflection:

Reorgs and restructuring may shake your confidence, but adaptability is a career superpower. When the dust settles, the question becomes: how do you know if you're still on track?

Let's Recap!

- Chaos doesn't mean failure—some disruption is normal in any reorg.

- Your job security may dip—be proactive with your work and relationships.

- You won't get all the answers. That's okay. Focus on what you can control.

- Use the 4Ps: Pause, Probe, Position, and Plan.

- Bullish professionals adapt. They don't fold. They realign and keep going.

9

CHAPTER

HOW AM I DOING?

As we discussed the employee experience through the Employee Lifecycle (see **Figure 1.2**), we have covered the following sections:

1. Onboarding & Assimilation

2. Performance & Development

The previous chapters cover topics such as getting feedback, developing skills, and tracking progress. However, what happens when you struggle with performance and do not deliver results?

In this chapter, we'll explore what happens when things don't go as planned, including how to identify performance challenges, seek support, and bounce back stronger.

WHEN PERFORMANCE STARTS TO SLIP

It's normal to underperform on occasion—everyone has an off quarter or even an off year from time to time. Despite the organization's desire for you to succeed, there may be times when coaching and mentoring are not enough to help you regain trust or meet expectations. Don't wait for a tough performance conversation to catch you off guard with your manager during the performance cycle; take proactive steps to address the issue.

When coaching and mentoring are not enough, it's essential to seek additional support. This might involve meeting with HR to discuss your challenges and exploring other resources the company offers. Many organizations provide access to training programs, employee assistance programs (EAPs), or even external coaching services. Taking the initiative to seek help demonstrates your commitment to improving and can provide you with new strategies and perspectives to address your performance issues.

When you find yourself struggling with performance, it's important to address the gaps head-on. Begin by having an open and honest conversation with your manager about your challenges. Ask for specific feedback on where you need improvement and discuss potential strategies to enhance your performance. This proactive approach shows your dedication to growth and willingness to take responsibility for your development.

A critical component of overcoming performance challenges is self-assessment and reflection. Take the time to honestly evaluate your strengths and weaknesses. Consider keeping a journal to document your daily activities, successes, and areas where you struggled. Reflecting on these entries can help you identify patterns and specific areas for improvement. Self-awareness is a powerful tool that can guide your efforts to enhance your performance and demonstrate to your employer that you are proactive in addressing your shortcomings.

Your colleagues can be valuable sources of feedback and support. Building strong working relationships and seeking input from your peers can provide you with different perspectives on your performance. Peer feedback can offer insights that you might not receive from managers alone and help you understand how your work impacts the team. Mentorship, whether formal or informal, can also be beneficial. A mentor can guide you through challenging times, offer constructive feedback, and help you navigate your career path more effectively.

Many organizations offer a range of resources to support employee development. Take advantage of online courses, in-house training sessions, and workshops that focus on the skills you need to improve. Additionally, consider joining professional organizations or networks related to your field. These resources can provide you with new insights, techniques, and the latest industry trends, helping you to stay competitive and competent in your role.

Often, performance issues can be traced back to poor time management. Assess how you allocate your time and identify any inefficiencies in your workflow. Techniques such as prioritizing tasks, creating to-do lists, and using time management tools can help you stay organized and focused. Effective time management enables you to meet deadlines consistently and reduces the stress associated with heavy workloads.

Effective communication is crucial in overcoming performance challenges. Ensure that you regularly update your manager on your progress and any difficulties that you encounter. Clear, concise communication helps manage expectations and fosters a supportive environment where issues can be addressed promptly. Additionally, improving your communication skills can enhance your overall performance and ability to collaborate with your team.

PAUL'S STORY

Turning Feedback into Action

Paul was a Product Marketing Associate at a computer networking company and reached out to me seeking advice about a potential career change. When I asked why he was considering leaving, he shared a surprising experience. "At my last performance review, my boss gave me incredibly positive feedback," Paul said. "But I was shocked to find out later that he had rated me as 'below average' on the formal performance scale."

I inquired about how he addressed this discrepancy. Paul admitted that he initially did nothing because he was unsure of the next steps. After discussing the situation with some colleagues, they encouraged him to have a follow-up conversation with his manager.

"I scheduled a meeting with my manager to understand why I received such a poor rating," Paul explained. "He told me, without much detail, that I was disengaged, didn't challenge myself, and lacked collaboration with others. He said, 'I expected more from you this year. You didn't seem as invested in the team's projects as you could have been.'"

Paul struggled to accept this feedback. "I don't agree with those points. I felt I was actively contributing and collaborating. If there were issues, he should have raised them earlier instead of waiting for the performance review. I was frustrated and angry during that meeting. I asked him, 'Can you give me specific examples of where I fell short? How can I address these concerns?'"

After a moment of reflection, Paul asked, "What should I do now?"

I recommended that Paul take a two-pronged approach. First, he should look for specific, actionable feedback from his manager about how he could improve in the areas mentioned. This would help him address any genuine concerns and demonstrate his willingness to grow. Second, I suggested he document his achievements and contributions to counterbalance the negative review and provide a clearer picture of his performance.

Paul took these steps seriously. He scheduled a follow-up meeting with his manager, asking for concrete examples and guidance on how to improve. "I requested detailed feedback and asked, 'Can you give me a list of actionable steps to work on?'" Additionally, he began keeping detailed records of his projects, accomplishments, and interactions with colleagues.

As weeks went by, Paul implemented the feedback he received, focusing on increased engagement and collaboration. He also continued to build relationships with his colleagues, actively seeking their input and feedback. For instance, he took on additional projects and participated more actively in team meetings.

Over time, Paul's efforts began to pay off. His manager acknowledged the improvements in a subsequent review, noting, "I've seen significant progress. Your increased engagement and collaboration have made a real difference." Paul felt more confident about his role and was pleased with the recognition of his hard work.

Ultimately, Paul chose to stay with the company. While a negative review can be disheartening, approaching it with a positive mindset and a clear plan for improvement can turn it into a pathway for future success. Like many employees that have faced similar challenges, Paul's experience, though tough, provided him with valuable insights into his professional strengths and areas for growth. Instead of giving up, he emerged more empowered and better equipped to handle future feedback constructively. This initiative-taking approach helps employees regain their standing within the organization with the hopes that their performance continues to improve.

These experiences not only strengthen resilience but also emphasize the importance of open communication and a commitment to continuous self-improvement when navigating career challenges.

WHEN YOU KNOW IT'S SERIOUS

If you're still struggling with your performance and your manager indicates that the situation is becoming more serious, you might notice several signs of a progressive corrective action process. This process typically begins with formal written warnings following initial coaching discussions. These warnings outline specific performance issues and set clear expectations for improvement. You'll likely experience increased monitoring of your work, including more frequent and structured feedback meetings.

A performance improvement plan with defined goals and deadlines will most likely be introduced and documented, and you may be required to participate in additional training or development.

Communication with your manager will likely become more formal, and your responsibilities may be adjusted to better align with your strengths. If improvements aren't made within a short period, your scope of responsibilities might be reduced. Throughout this process, your manager will closely document your performance issues and progress, aiming to support your development while addressing ongoing concerns. Recognizing these signs can help you understand what is happening and how to respond.

In my experience as a Human Resources Executive, collaborating with both new and seasoned managers to address performance issues is vital. Surprisingly, many managers avoid confronting these issues due to discomfort or a desire to avoid conflict, which can lead to unresolved problems. It is vital for managers to understand and implement an effective progressive discipline process, which involves addressing performance concerns head-on, setting clear improvement goals, and taking proactive steps to prevent future problems. This process should cultivate a culture of respect and accountability, where all employees are consistently held to high standards and supported in their development.

For a recent hire, this experience might be new in the workplace but may feel familiar if you struggled during college. In college, facing poor grades and academic challenges is not uncommon and can be discouraging. However, you didn't give up; you refocused, addressed the issues, and got back on track. The workplace is similar. Just as you had to manage class preparation, deadlines, and competing demands in college, you'll need to apply the same resilience and problem-solving skills at work.

Workplace struggles can be addressed using strategies to help you recover. The following section will help you realize that struggling at work is as common as struggling in college and that you can overcome it. Remember, a rough patch academically wasn't the end of your college career, and it's certainly not the end of your professional career. Work hard, follow the advice above, and you'll be on the road to recovery before you know it.

⚲AN INSIDER'S VIEW ⚲

Most companies in most industries have what they call a 'Progressive Discipline Policy' in place for both employees and managers to adhere to. It's a policy designed to address unacceptable behavior or poor performance through a structured process that escalates consequences if issues are not resolved (see **Figure 9.1**). This approach ensures that employees are given clear opportunities to improve while providing a fair and consistent method for managing performance issues.

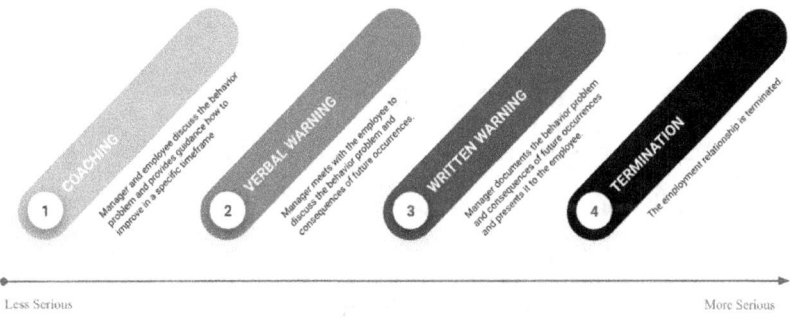

Figure 9.1: Steps of Progressive Discipline

What Is Progressive Discipline?

Progressive discipline (also known as 'Progressive Correction Action') is a process used by employers to address unacceptable behavior or poor performance when coaching and support are insufficient. This approach involves escalating consequences if the employee's behavior or performance does not meet established standards. The goal is to correct behavior by clearly communicating issues and providing opportunities for improvement.[29] If you start noticing early signs of this process with your manager, don't panic—there's still time to remedy the situation.

Typical behaviors that may trigger progressive discipline include:

- Failure to meet job requirements
- Missing deadlines
- Poor work quality
- Unexcused absences
- Tardiness
- Misuse of company property
- Fighting with others (physical or verbal)
- Sexual harassment
- Creating a hostile work environment
- Insubordination
- Lack of engagement with others
- Poor teamwork

The process typically involves documenting each step and reinforcing the seriousness of the issue. For most companies, common steps include verbal warning, written warning, and termination. However, severe misconduct may necessitate skipping some steps. HR departments should establish clear procedures and consult with an employment attorney or experienced HR professional when termination is a consideration.

Employer Benefits of a Progressive Discipline Process

Not all employees understand why such a process is in place. A business stands to benefit in multiple ways by adopting a progressive discipline process as part of the Employee Handbook or other key company policies. Taking these proactive measures can help you:

1. **Promote a Culture of Open Communication**: By fostering a system where managers and employees can openly discuss performance and behavior, you create a supportive environment. This openness encourages employees to seek feedback and guidance, leading to more opportunities for coaching and mentoring. As a result, employees feel more valued and understood, which can enhance their engagement and commitment to the organization.

2. **Increase Employee Retention**: Addressing issues early on through coaching or progressive discipline can resolve problems before they escalate to the point of no return - termination. This approach helps employees understand what is expected of them and provides the support they need to improve. By correcting behavior and performance issues promptly, you reduce turnover and retain valuable talent, saving the costs associated with hiring and training new employees.

3. **Provide Important Documentation**: A well-documented progressive discipline process ensures that all steps taken to address an employee's performance or behavior issues are recorded. This documentation is crucial if termination becomes necessary, as it provides evidence that the employer took reasonable steps to help the employee improve. It also protects the organization in case of legal disputes, demonstrating that the termination was justified and handled fairly.

4. **Enhance Managerial Effectiveness**: Progressive discipline helps managers address performance and behavior issues systematically. By following a structured approach, managers can achieve higher performance and productivity from their teams. Clear guidelines and expectations reduce ambiguity, enabling managers to lead more effectively and confidently.

5. **Recognize Good Performance and Address Poor Performance**: Implementing a progressive discipline process at a company level sends a clear message that the organization values high performance and will address poor performance. This balance reinforces the importance of meeting standards and contributes to a culture where employees are motivated to excel, knowing their efforts will be recognized and appreciated.

6. **Ensure Consistency and Fairness**: A standardized discipline process ensures that all employees are treated consistently and fairly. This uniformity helps to prevent

favoritism or bias, promoting a sense of equity within the organization. Employees are more likely to trust the system and feel secure in their roles when they know that everyone is held to the same standards.

7. **Facilitate Defensible Terminations**: When an employee does not improve despite the progressive discipline process, the organization can conduct a fair, documented, and defensible termination. This thorough approach minimizes the risk of wrongful termination claims and reinforces the organization's commitment to maintaining a productive and respectful workplace.

Believe me when I say that no one looks forward to having challenging performance conversations at work—these discussions are uncomfortable for both managers and employees. However, following a structured process can make these difficult conversations more manageable. By integrating a progressive discipline process, employers can address performance and behavior issues constructively, leading to a more engaged, productive, and cohesive workforce.

What Are the Steps for a Progressive Discipline Process?

As a Human Resources Executive, I frequently encounter surprises from employees who are terminated for performance issues, with common reactions such as, "*I didn't realize there was a performance problem*" or "*My manager never communicated the severity of the issue.*" Even when managers have documented evidence of performance-related conversations, such reactions indicate a possible communication gap or a lack of understanding of the seriousness of the performance issue. To address this, it is crucial to thoroughly understand the progressive discipline process. By familiarizing yourself with this process, you can better navigate any performance issues, giving you the opportunity to improve your standing with the company before it's too late.

As shown in **Figure 9.1**, the progressive discipline process involves a structured series of steps to address employee issues, starting with initial coaching conversations and potentially leading to termination. This approach ensures that performance and behavior issues are managed systematically, with clear documentation of each step, helping both employees and employers manage and resolve issues effectively.

1. Verbal Warning

If you have had several coaching sessions with your manager but have not seen improvements in your performance, the next step is a verbal warning. This step formalizes the discussion and provides an opportunity for corrective action. Although the warning is delivered verbally, it is essential to document the conversation to create a record.

Key details to include are:

- The date and time of the verbal warning.
- The specific issues discussed, and the improvements required.
- The next steps agreed upon during the meeting.

- The names of those present during the conversation.

If you find yourself in this situation, I strongly recommend documenting the conversation yourself and not relying on your manager to summarize the details of the conversation. This ensures that the discussion and agreements regarding expectations, actions, and timelines are accurately recorded, providing you with a clear reference and protecting your interests.

2. Written Warning

If the verbal warning does not lead to the desired improvement after 30 or 60 days, a formal written warning follows. This is also referred to as a PIP (Performance Improvement Plan). A manager may issue multiple written warnings for certain infractions.

A written warning typically includes:

- Details of the policy or performance expectations in question.

- A description of how the employee's actions violated company rules or failed to meet expectations.

- An action plan with specific steps for improvement.

- The potential disciplinary actions if no improvement is observed.

- The date of the written warning and signatures of all parties present.

During the meeting where the written warning is issued, you as the employee should have the chance to provide feedback. It is important to clarify that signing the document does not imply agreement but acknowledges that the discussion took place, and the employee understands the corrective actions required. The signed document is usually sent to HR or added to your personnel file.

3. Final Warning

The final warning represents the last opportunity for you as the employee to correct their performance or behavior. This step makes it clear that without measurable improvement, termination is the next step. In some cases, companies may also involve suspension with or without pay.

Documentation should:

- Restate the policy or performance expectation.
- Clearly outline the issue, required improvements, and consequences of further non-compliance.
- Indicate that this is the final warning.

The document should be filed with HR along with any previous warnings.

4. Termination of Employment

Termination, though a last resort, may become necessary if previous disciplinary steps do not yield the desired improvements. To ensure that the process is conducted smoothly and fairly, consider the following steps:

- Ensure that the final decision to terminate is clear.

- Have a witness present during the termination meeting such as HR.

- Review the progressive discipline process with the employee, referencing all prior documentation.

- Be prepared for the employee's reaction.

- Provide a written, dated termination notice, have all parties sign it, and retain the original for your records.

- Prepare your final paycheck and address the termination of benefits.

- Review state or local regulations related to termination.

- Collect any company property, such as key fobs, laptops, and other equipment.

- Maintain confidentiality throughout the process.

By the time you reach the termination stage, the outcome should not come as a surprise. The progressive discipline process is designed to give employees multiple opportunities to improve and to clearly communicate the seriousness of performance issues.[30] If termination becomes necessary, it indicates that the concerns were consistently addressed and documented over time. Employees should recognize that this step is a culmination of ongoing discussions and efforts to rectify the issues. A well-documented and transparent process ensures that termination is a last resort after all other avenues have been exhausted.

🐃 Let's Be Bullish:

IF TERMINATION FEELS IMMINENT

Facing performance issues or the possibility of termination really sucks. It's especially daunting for recent college graduates or those just entering the workforce. Most people don't imagine being fired when they start a new job—especially early in their careers.

The prospect of termination is often an overlooked aspect of launching a career. It's natural to worry about the impact on your resume, LinkedIn profile, or how others might perceive you if you lose your job. These concerns are both valid and common among those new to professional settings. However, confronting these realities head-on is essential.

Addressing performance issues early and proactively can help mitigate potential negative outcomes. If you suspect that termination might be imminent due to performance issues, it's important to take a strategic approach. Consider taking the following steps:

1. **Review Your Performance Documentation**: Carefully review any performance evaluations, warnings, and feedback you have received. Ensure you understand the specific areas where your performance has been deemed unsatisfactory.

2. **Seek Clarification**: If you haven't already, request a meeting with your manager or HR to discuss your performance issues and clarify expectations. This can provide you with a final opportunity to address any concerns or misunderstandings.

3. **Develop a Plan for Improvement**: Create a detailed plan to address the areas where your performance has fallen

short. Set clear, measurable goals and outline steps you can take to improve. Share this plan with your manager to demonstrate your commitment to making changes.

4. **Request Additional Support**: Ask your manager or HR for additional training, coaching, or tools to help you improve your performance, ask for them. Showing that you are proactive and willing to invest in your own development can positively impact your situation.

5. **Document Your Efforts**: Keep detailed records of your attempts to improve, including any additional work, training, or steps you have taken. This documentation can be valuable if you need to defend your actions or negotiate terms.

6. **Consider Alternative Solutions**: Explore if there are other roles or departments within the company where your skills might be a better fit. If so, express your interest in transferring rather than being terminated.

7. **Prepare for a Possible Termination**: Start preparing for the possibility of termination by updating your resume, LinkedIn profile, and networking with industry contacts. Begin looking for new job opportunities as a contingency plan.

8. **Know Your Rights**: Familiarize yourself with your company's policies and any relevant labor laws regarding termination. Understanding your rights can help you navigate the process more effectively.

9. **Seek Legal Advice**: If you suspect that the termination process may not be handled fairly or if you have concerns about your legal rights, consult with an employment attorney to get professional advice.

10. **Focus on Your Well-Being**: The prospect of termination can be stressful. Take care of your mental and physical health, and seek support from friends, family, or a counselor if needed.

No one likes to talk about it, but losing employment due to poor performance is disheartening. However, it can also be an opportunity for growth. This setback allows you to reflect on your experience, adjust your job search strategy, and approach new opportunities with renewed vigor. By understanding your situation and preparing for future possibilities, you can effectively navigate this difficult transitional period.

Here are some tips for moving forward after being terminated.

UNDERSTAND THE REALITY OF YOUR SITUATION

1. **Reflect on Your Firing:** Analyze the reasons for your dismissal and consider any contributing factors. Understanding these can help you identify areas for improvement and avoid repeating past mistakes.

2. **Deal with Your Emotions:** Acknowledge and process your emotions, such as anger or shame, to move forward effectively. Engage in healthy coping mechanisms like talking to a trusted friend or seeking professional help if needed.

3. **Identify Your Mistakes:** Recognize specific mistakes that led to poor performance. This helps you understand your strengths and weaknesses, create a plan for improvement, and demonstrate growth to potential employers.

Preparation for Future Opportunities

1. **Develop an Improvement Plan:** Address the reasons behind your dismissal by identifying areas for improvement, setting achievable goals, and assessing progress regularly.

2. **Acquire New Skills:** Stay competitive by attending workshops, conferences, online courses, and networking events. Practice new skills to reinforce learning.

3. **Consider Further Education or Certifications:** Pursue relevant degrees or certifications to show commitment to personal growth and enhance your career prospects.

By reflecting on your experience and proactively addressing past errors, you can regain confidence and present yourself as a strong candidate for future job opportunities.

BULLISH PRO TIPS

- **Own your performance narrative.** Don't wait for reviews—track your progress weekly and reflect monthly.

- **Ask early, not after the fact.** Don't wait until review season to ask how you're doing—get ahead of it.

- **Document everything.** Projects, wins, feedback—your personal performance log is your best defense and amplifier.
- **Address misalignment fast.** If you feel blindsided by feedback, speak up. Don't assume silence means approval.
- **Stay curious, not defensive.** Performance dips happen—how you respond determines what happens next.

Closing Reflection:

Performance struggles don't define your career — your response does. When you perform well, recognition often follows in the form of rewards and pay.

Let's Recap!

If You're Struggling Now...

- **Initiate a Constructive Dialogue**: Address performance issues early by having an open, honest conversation with your manager.
- **Develop an Actionable Improvement Plan**: Collaborate with your manager to set specific goals and clear steps for improvement.
- **Understand the Progressive Discipline Process**: Know that many companies follow a structured and escalating approach to performance issues, giving you time and opportunity to course correct.

If You've Been Let Go...

- **Prepare for New Opportunities**: Reflect on your experience, extract the lessons, and shift your focus to what's next. Use this as a springboard to recalibrate your goals and rebuild stronger.

10

CHAPTER

SHOW ME THE MONEY!

The iconic line – SHOW ME THE MONY!!! — from the movie *Jerry Maguire*—perfectly captures how most employees feel when it comes to compensation. As you progress within an organization, stage four of the Employee Lifecycle—Total Rewards & Retention—takes center stage (see **Figure 1.2**).

For new hires, salary adjustments often hinge on performance, which varies by company and industry. That leads to a crucial question: *What does your company actually consider 'merit,' and how is it measured?*

Understanding the specific criteria used to evaluate your performance and how it impacts your compensation is essential.

By proactively seeking clarity on these factors, you can navigate your career path more effectively, ensuring your contributions are recognized and appropriately rewarded. Take charge of your professional journey by discussing these criteria with your manager and utilizing available resources to advocate for the compensation you deserve.

Am I getting paid fairly? Are others in similar roles earning more than I am? These questions can trigger anxiety, especially when you suspect your contributions aren't being reflected in your paycheck—or when peers in similar roles seem to be earning more. It's natural to focus more on your compensation as you gain experience within the organization. While there isn't a universal formula for determining fair pay, several key factors and strategies can guide you in evaluating whether your salary is reasonable.

Industry Standards: Begin by researching salary benchmarks for your role within your specific industry and geographic region. Utilize resources such as Glassdoor, Payscale, and LinkedIn Salary Insights, which offer comprehensive data on what others in similar positions are earning. By comparing your salary to these benchmarks, you can gain insight into whether your compensation is aligned with industry norms.

Company's Compensation Policies: As an employee, understanding your company's compensation policies is crucial, as they are guided by the organization's 'Rewards Philosophy.' This philosophy encompasses the principles and strategies that guide how a company compensates and recognizes employees. It reflects how an organization aligns its reward system with its overall business goals, values, and culture.[31] Key aspects of a company's rewards philosophy typically include:

- **Alignment with Business Objectives:** The rewards philosophy should support the company's strategic goals and drive behaviors that contribute to its success.

- **Fairness and Equity:** Ensuring rewards are distributed fairly and equitably, with clear criteria for performance-based rewards and consistent application.

- **Competitiveness:** Maintaining compensation packages that attract and retain talent by regularly benchmarking salaries and benefits against industry standards.

- **Recognition of Performance:** Emphasizing the importance of recognizing and rewarding individual and team achievements through performance bonuses, promotions, and other forms of acknowledgment.

- **Development and Growth:** Incorporating opportunities for professional development, skill enhancement, and career advancement as part of the rewards system.

- **Employee Engagement and Satisfaction:** Enhancing engagement and satisfaction by providing meaningful rewards and recognition to boost morale and motivation.

- **Transparency and Communication:** Clearly communicating how rewards are determined and distributed, helping employees understand expectations and how their performance impacts their compensation.

- **Flexibility and Adaptability:** Being open to revising reward structures to address changing market trends, employee needs, and organizational changes.

- **Peer Data:** To remain competitive, a company may identify a list of companies within their industry and benchmark against them to assess the competitiveness and appropriateness of the overall rewards programs.

Performance Metrics: Understand how your performance is evaluated and its impact on your pay. Many companies implement performance-based salary structures that reward employees for achieving specific goals or contributing to organizational success (see **Figure 10.1**). Clear performance metrics can guide you in understanding how your accomplishments might influence your salary adjustments. However, it's important to note that salary increases are not guaranteed. Managers consider factors such as relative performance, current salary compared to the salary midpoint, market data for the position, and approved budgets.

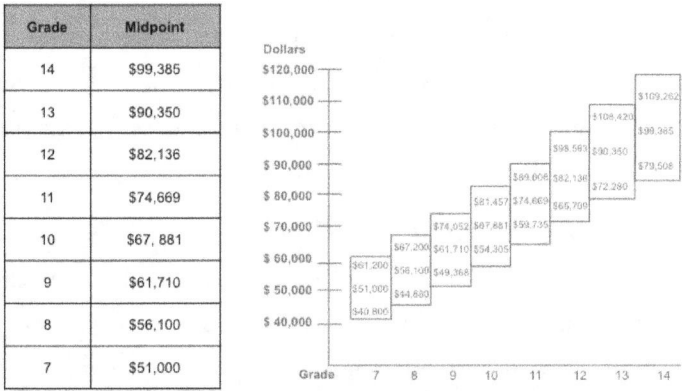

Grade	Midpoint
14	$99,385
13	$90,350
12	$82,136
11	$74,669
10	$67, 881
9	$61,710
8	$56,100
7	$51,000

Figure 10.1: Salary Structure and Ranges

219

Experience and Skills: Reflect on your experience, skills, and educational background. Your compensation should correspond to your level of expertise and specialized skills. Comparing your qualifications with others in similar roles can help ensure that your salary is appropriate for your experience and skill set. Specialized skills or advanced certifications may justify higher compensation.

Negotiation Opportunities: Evaluate whether you've had the chance to discuss your salary expectations with your employer. Many employees hesitate to initiate open discussions about compensation with their managers, often opting instead to explore external job opportunities for a higher salary. However, addressing salary adjustments or promotion opportunities internally can be more effective and beneficial in the long run.

Before exploring external opportunities, consider having a constructive conversation with your manager about your current compensation. Effective negotiation, backed by a clear demonstration of your value and contributions to the company, can sometimes lead to better compensation packages and career advancement within your current organization. Engaging in this dialogue shows your commitment to growth and provides a chance to align your compensation with your performance and contributions.

While a precise formula for fair pay doesn't exist, evaluating these factors will provide you with a clearer understanding of whether your compensation is in line with market standards and your professional worth.[32] By using salary comparison tools, understanding your company's policies, and engaging in open discussions with your employer, you can work towards ensuring that your salary is fair and reflective of your contributions. A proactive approach to assessing and negotiating your salary not only helps you secure equitable compensation but also fosters a more transparent and fulfilling career trajectory.

TYPES OF PAY STRUCTURES

Understanding the framework of a salary structure and your position within it helps you gauge where you stand compared to the market, as illustrated in **Figure 10.1**. For example, graded (or traditional) salary structures are widely used by companies to manage employee compensation.[33] These structures feature a clear hierarchy of job grades or levels, each associated with a specific salary range. They are prevalent across many industries due to their effectiveness and straightforward approach.

In a graded salary structure, employees typically advance through the salary range over time based on performance, experience, and tenure. This progression rewards and retains employees as they develop their skills and gain experience. For instance, roles might be designated as UX Designer I, II, or III, with each level offering a distinct salary range that increases with each promotion.

In contrast, broadband salary structures provide a different approach. They involve fewer pay grades with broader salary ranges, allowing for greater flexibility in compensation. This structure enables organizations to accommodate a wider range of salaries within fewer levels, offering more leeway in salary adjustments. For employees, this means more variation in pay among peers at the same level—so it's even more important to understand what drives your individual compensation.

Market-based pay structures use external market data to set salary levels for various job positions. This method helps organizations align their compensation strategies with industry standards and the external labor market, ensuring competitive and fair pay.

Step structures, another compensation model, define pay based on predetermined grades with incremental steps within each grade. Employees start at the initial step and advance to higher steps based on performance and tenure, receiving salary increases as they progress. While step structures provide a clear and organized framework, they are less flexible compared to other models.

Each of these salary structures has its own advantages and limitations.[34] Understanding the difference and which one your company models after can help you navigate your career and manage your compensation expectations effectively.

POSITION WITHIN A PAY STRUCTURE

Different pay structures reflect a company's rewards philosophy, balancing competitive compensation with fairness. Understanding your place within the company's salary range is crucial for knowing how to progress based on your performance or meet the requirements for promotion.[35]

A typical salary range consists of a minimum, midpoint, and maximum:

- Minimum: The lowest amount an employee in the role will earn.

- Midpoint: The middle of the pay band, often aligned with the market median based on salary surveys.

- Maximum: The highest rate of pay an employee in the role may expect to earn.

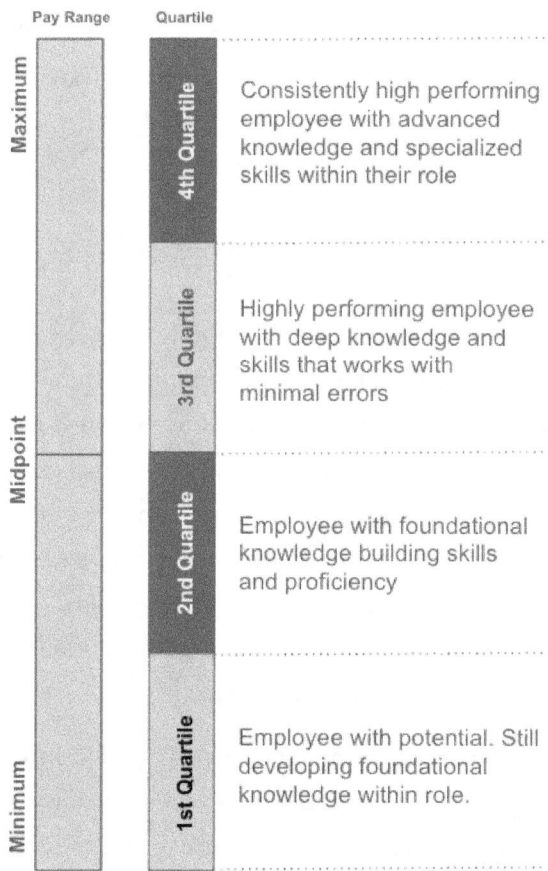

Figure 10.2: Salary Structure with Quartiles

223

Figure 10.2 illustrates how employees are typically positioned within a salary range—from minimum to maximum—based on their skills, experience, and performance.

- Employees still developing in their roles may earn between the minimum and midpoint.

- Proficient employees, who complete work independently and accurately, are typically paid closer to the midpoint.

- High-performing employees, who demonstrate significant independence and excellence, will find their pay between the midpoint and maximum.

As a recent graduate, you should expect to be in the 1st or 2nd quartile of your assigned salary range. As you participate in your company's merit process, you will be eligible for salary increases based on your overall performance. Companies often use market data from third-party compensation firms to establish each salary range and may differentiate pay between non-technical and technical roles. For example, a company might set the 50th percentile of market data as the midpoint for non-technical roles and the 65th percentile for technical roles. Each grade level reflects job scope and responsibilities, and each salary range is aligned with the external market for talent.

Many companies maintain transparency around compensation and encourage open dialogue with managers—typically during the company's performance reviews and salary discussions, others may not have fully developed structures, making their compensation practices appear inconsistent or ambiguous.[36]

MITCH'S STORY

Let's Talk About Money

Mitch was a Customer Success Associate for a cybersecurity company. He had always been a model employee since he started as a new college graduate. His colleagues admired his dedication, and his manager, Sarah, appreciated his consistent performance over the last two years. Despite the positive feedback, Mitch harbored a lingering concern: his salary.

Growing up, Mitch was taught that discussing money was taboo. Conversations about finances were considered impolite and, often, downright rude. His parents had always emphasized that salaries were private matters to be kept secret and never shared. As a result, Mitch never quite knew how to broach the subject of compensation, even with the reassurance of his own hard work.

One chilly Monday morning, Mitch was called into Sarah's office. He knew the meeting was about his performance review, but his anxiety about discussing his salary clouded his focus. As he sat across from Sarah, her warm smile did little to quell his unease.

Sarah began the meeting with praise, highlighting Mitch's impressive contributions over the past year. "Mitch," she started, "your dedication and hard work have not gone unnoticed. Your performance this year has been outstanding, and I'm grateful for your commitment." Mitch felt a mix of pride and apprehension as Sarah transitioned to discussing salary adjustments. The conversation, though necessary, was an uncomfortable departure from the usual focus on performance.

Sarah noticed Mitch's discomfort and decided to address it directly. "Mitch," she said gently, "I understand that talking about money can feel awkward, but it's an important part of your career growth. Let's address it openly and honestly. It's essential that you feel valued and clear about how your compensation reflects your contributions."

Mitch took a deep breath, realizing that this was his chance to overcome the discomfort he had grown up with. "I appreciate your honesty, Sarah," he began, "and I agree that we need to discuss my compensation. I've been dedicated to my role and would like to understand how my salary reflects that."

Sarah nodded, relieved by Mitch's willingness to engage in the conversation. "Absolutely, Mitch. Your performance has been excellent, and we want to ensure that your compensation aligns with both your contributions and market standards. Let's review how your role and achievements fit into our compensation structure."

They discussed Mitch's performance, market standards, and how his contributions aligned with the company's compensation structure. Sarah explained, "Given your performance and the current market rates, we believe you are due for a salary adjustment. However, we also want to set clear goals for the upcoming year to ensure your continued growth and alignment with our strategic objectives."

Mitch listened intently, feeling more at ease as the discussion became more constructive. Sarah continued, "I'd also like to offer you opportunities for further professional development. We have several training programs and leadership development initiatives that could benefit you. Let's work together to identify areas where you can grow and how we can support you in achieving your career aspirations."

As the meeting concluded, Mitch felt a weight lifted off his shoulders. The conversation had been challenging, but it had also been enlightening. Mitch realized that discussing salary did not have to be a difficult subject. With Sarah's guidance, he had navigated a difficult dialogue and emerged with a clearer understanding of his value to the company.

Sarah wrapped up the meeting with encouragement, "Mitch, I appreciate your openness in this discussion. It's important that we keep transparency and support your career growth. Let's schedule regular check-ins to ensure we're on track and to address any concerns you may have."

In the end, Mitch's willingness to tackle the uncomfortable topic had not only provided clarity for himself but had also strengthened his working relationship with Sarah. Mitch learned that while conversations about compensation might always carry some discomfort, addressing them openly was a crucial part of professional growth.

Mitch's experience highlights the importance for employees to understand where they stand in relation to their company's salary ranges and levels. Many employees, much like Mitch, are often hesitant to broach the subject of compensation due to societal norms that label such discussions as inappropriate or awkward. However, gaining clarity on where your pay aligns with the company's compensation structure (see **Figure 10.1**) allows you to assess whether you are being fairly compensated for your skills, experience, and contributions.

Knowing your position within the salary range can help you identify any discrepancies and address them, ensuring that you are not undervalued or underpaid or perhaps address any performance concerns that may exist (see **Figure 10.3**).

Lower Quartile	Midpoint	Upper Quartile
Employee with less work experience or new to role	Employees with critical skills, but there is not a shortage of talent in the job market	Employees in key positions in the organization and/or have critical skills that have limited supply in the job market
Employees that have minimum qualifications to fulfill the job responsibilities	Employees that are fully qualified for the job	Employees with higher qualifications that the job requires
Employee not meeting the minimum performance requirement for the job	Employees that meet the established performance criteria for the job	Employees that exceed established performance criteria

Figure 10.3: Salary Structure Position and Definition

This knowledge of salary range position empowers you to make informed decisions about your career and financial future. Additionally, it encourages you to have these important conversations with your manager, who can provide insights and support for your compensation concerns, rather than prematurely exploring external opportunities solely for financial reasons.

Understanding your company's salary structure also helps you set realistic and attainable career goals. When you are aware of the pay scales and what is needed to move up within them, you can more effectively plan your professional development and advancement. Engaging in open discussions with your manager about your compensation and career trajectory fosters a transparent and fair workplace culture.

This proactive approach not only enhances your own career satisfaction but also strengthens your commitment to your current organization. Employees who are informed about their compensation and career progression are more engaged, motivated, and less likely to seek external opportunities out of financial frustration. Therefore, before considering a move to another company for a higher salary, it is important to explore and address your compensation concerns within your current organization. This can lead to a more fulfilling and stable career path, benefiting both you and your employer.

THE MONEY TALK

When it's time to talk salary, preparation is everything. And just as important as what you *do* say—is what you *don't*. Below are common missteps that can derail the conversation or weaken your credibility.

"I need a raise because I have bills to pay."

Your personal expenses aren't part of your employer's compensation philosophy. Stick to performance, market data, and value—not lifestyle costs.

"I heard [Insert Coworker's Name] makes more than me."

Avoid referencing someone else's pay unless your company practices full salary transparency. Instead, focus on your own contributions, market benchmarks, and where you fall in your pay band.

"I've been here X months—don't I automatically get a raise?"

Raises aren't tied to time served; they're tied to impact. Show how your work has driven results, not just how long you've occupied your seat.

"If I don't get a raise, I'm going to start looking elsewhere."

Threats rarely land well and can damage trust. Instead, express your desire to grow with the company—and ask how you can increase your value moving forward.

"I think I *deserve* more."

That word—*deserve*—can feel emotional or subjective. Swap it with "based on my contributions, I'd like to discuss how my compensation aligns with expectations and market data."

BULLISH PRO TIP

Frame your ask around your **impact**, **performance**, and **market alignment**—not emotion, entitlement, or hearsay. Be calm, confident, and prepared with data.

⚲AN INSIDER'S VIEW ⚲

Money isn't everything, particularly when it comes to selecting or maintaining a career. While competitive salaries are crucial for attracting and keeping top talent, they represent only one aspect of what makes a company a great place to work. Employee benefits, workplace culture, office environment, and other intangible perks also significantly enhance your business's appeal to potential employees and foster loyalty among your current workforces.

Not all employees realize that 'total rewards' encompass both monetary and non-monetary aspects, including benefits, pay, and awards received throughout their tenure with a company. For an organization, a total rewards strategy represents a comprehensive approach to employee compensation that goes beyond mere salary and wages.[37] It includes a range of financial and non-financial rewards designed to recognize and value employees' contributions and loyalty. This strategy aims to attract, retain, and motivate top talent by offering a competitive and balanced rewards package that aligns with employees' diverse needs and preferences. Key elements often include base pay, incentive pay, benefits, time off, work-life balance programs, professional development opportunities, recognition programs, and various employee perks.

A strategic focus on compensation is crucial for companies aiming to build a strong, motivated, and committed workforce. Even though total rewards vary by industry, compensation remains a cornerstone of employee engagement and retention. While every company's approach may differ, investing in a competitive and equitable compensation strategy demonstrates to employees that their contributions are valued and that the organization is committed to their well-being.[38] This investment can lead to enhanced job satisfaction, lower turnover rates, and a more positive work environment, ultimately contributing to the company's long-term success.

The importance of focusing on compensation also lies in its direct impact on a company's ability to compete in the talent market. In today's competitive job landscape, attracting and retaining skilled professionals requires more than just a good salary. Candidates are looking for a comprehensive rewards package that includes benefits, work-life balance, and opportunities for career growth. Companies that prioritize and effectively manage compensation can differentiate themselves from competitors, securing top talent and enhancing their reputation as an employer of choice.

As an employee, it's important to recognize that a well-structured compensation strategy aligns your efforts with organizational goals. When compensation is linked to performance metrics and achievements, it enhances motivation to meet targets and drives the company's success. This alignment ensures that both organizational and employee interests are mutually beneficial, boosting productivity and cultivating a sense of ownership and loyalty.

Equally important is employee recognition within a successful total rewards model. While material incentives are valuable, acknowledging employees' hard work through individual awards or titles—such as Employee of the Month or achievement awards—can greatly enhance engagement and morale. This recognition helps reinforce employees' commitment and contributions, making them feel valued and integral to the company's success.

Many companies invest heavily in their Total Rewards Programs because a strategic focus on compensation is critical for attracting and retaining top talent. It also plays a key role in enhancing job satisfaction and motivating employees to contribute to organizational success.[39] By offering a competitive and well-rounded compensation package, companies not only improve their ability to attract skilled professionals but also foster a more engaged and committed workforce. This, in turn, supports long-term success and growth.

According to a recent survey, 9 out of 10 employees desire more than just an annual salary increase; they want meaningful recognition and rewards for their hard work.[40] Implementing a holistic approach to rewards—including comprehensive benefits and recognition programs—can lead to a more engaged workforce and improved employee retention rates.

🐂 Let's Be Bullish:

As you move forward in your career, you'll naturally learn more about compensation—whether through review cycles, promotions, or simply switching companies. For new hires, these conversations may feel daunting at first, but rest assured: that's normal.

By now, you've gained a solid understanding of how total rewards work. So, what's next?

Start by aligning your performance with your company's pay-for-performance model. These systems link compensation to results through formal goal-setting and reviews. They're designed to reward high performers, keep salaries competitive, and ensure compensation is an investment—not a handout. (see **Figure 10.4).**

By increasing pay only when performance justifies it, companies avoid over-investing in underperformers and instead focus their resources on employees who contribute meaningfully to business success. This approach motivates individuals to do their best work while ensuring compensation dollars are used wisely.

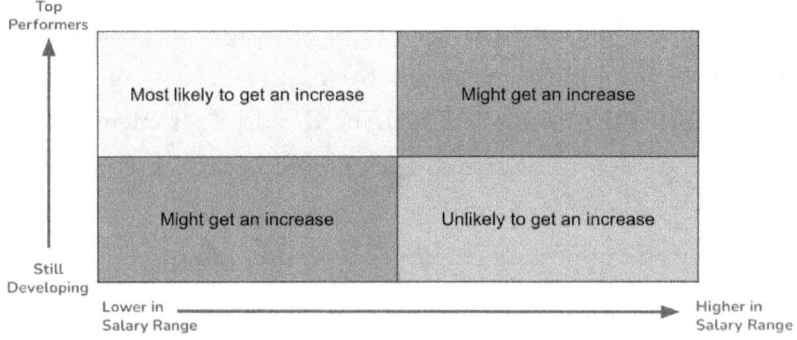

Figure 10.4: Performance vs. Salary Range Position

Understanding where you fall on this grid—based on your current salary and performance—can help you anticipate salary adjustments and better prepare for merit conversations.

Grasping how the pay-for-performance model works is especially valuable early in your career. It helps you connect your contributions to compensation in a clear and structured way. But to benefit fully, your goals must be relevant, measurable, and achievable.

For those motivated by financial growth, mastering this framework and fully engaging in the review process can be a game-changer. When employees understand how compensation decisions are made and how they can influence outcomes, they become more focused, aligned, and empowered.

Take proactive steps:

- Familiarize yourself with your company's compensation structure.
- Clarify the expectations tied to your role and salary band.
- Have regular conversations with your manager about performance, growth areas, and what it takes to move up—either within your current salary range or to the next grade level.

These discussions aren't just about money—they're about your development, value, and career trajectory. Addressing them head-on not only builds your confidence but also contributes to a more transparent and productive workplace culture.

By strategically managing your development and aligning your performance with company expectations, you can unlock greater earning potential and long-term success within your organization.

BULLISH PRO TIPS

- **Know your company's compensation calendar.** Merit cycles, review periods, and bonus timelines matter—plan your ask accordingly.

- **Do your homework.** Use Glassdoor, Salary.com Levels.fyi, and industry reports to understand market rates for your role and location.

- **Understand your salary range.** Ask where you fall in your pay band and what it takes to move up.

- **Talk compensation early—professionally.** It's okay to ask, "Can we review how compensation aligns with my performance?"

- **Don't just chase the number.** Total rewards include benefits, learning, growth, and flexibility—factor it all in.

- **Pay transparency is growing.** If your company has published salary bands or levels, review them and ask your manager for context if they're unclear.

Closing Reflection

Pay is more than numbers—it's philosophy, structure, and perceived value. But compensation alone isn't enough; what matters just as much is whether you feel valued day to day.

Let's Recap!

- **Understand the 'Rewards Philosophy':** Familiarize yourself with your company's compensation policies to accelerate your career growth and maximize your potential within the organization.

- **Align Goals with Company Objectives:** Grasping key aspects of the rewards philosophy helps you navigate career development and align your personal goals with company objectives.

- **Appreciate the Holistic Compensation Approach:** Recognize that total rewards include both financial and non-financial elements designed to attract, keep, and motivate top talent.

- **Strategically Plan Career Moves:** Understand the criteria for promotions and salary increases so you can make informed decisions about your next steps.

PART THREE: EARN YOUR WINGS

Key Takeaways

NOTES:_____

_____

_____

_____

_____

_____

_____

ACTIONS:_____

_____

_____

_____

_____

_____

_____

_____

Pause & Reflect

Before You Enter Part Four – Path Unlocked

At this stage, you've likely felt both momentum and friction. Maybe you've been calibrated behind closed doors, learned the compensation game, or faced tough feedback. You've earned some strips—and maybe some scars.

Take a moment to reflect:

- What's your current reputation inside the company?

- Are you on anyone's radar as a high performer?

- Have you built working relationships that will advocate for you—whether you stay or go?

The final chapters will push you to evaluate your value, your career options, and your exit strategy—on your terms.

PART FOUR

PATH UNLOCKED

"Doors open with experience"

11

CHAPTER

————

THE HIDDEN LADDER

Here's a little secret: not every open position needs to be filled with an external hire. As someone new to the corporate world, you've probably noticed a few colleagues moving into new roles, joining a different team, or even transferring to a new department entirely. Depending on your organization's size and maturity, you may not have heard the term 'internal mobility,' but you've likely seen it in action.

Internal mobility refers to the movement of current employees—upward, laterally, or into new roles—within the same company. These opportunities can take many forms: promotions, interdepartmental transfers, project-based assignments, mentorship programs, and job shadowing experiences. Each path allows employees to explore new career directions without leaving the organization.

The good news? Internal mobility is no longer rare. Many companies now prioritize this approach as a way to fill skill gaps, increase retention, and promote agility[41]. The better news? As a high-performing early-career professional, you can absolutely position yourself to take advantage of it.

SO, WHAT DOES THIS LOOK LIKE IN REAL LIFE?

Sometimes internal mobility doesn't begin with a formal job posting—it starts with a question. A moment of curiosity. A desire to grow.

Lia's story captures just that. As an early-career professional, she didn't wait for an invitation. She started the conversation, and what followed was a powerful example of how performance, visibility, and courage can unlock new opportunities from within.

LIA'S STORY

Taking a Big Leap Forward

Lia had been in her role as a Business Operations Associate for just over a year. She was reliable, sharp, and known for her detailed dashboards that helped cross-functional teams stay on track. But lately, she felt like she had mastered her day-to-day tasks. *What's next?* she wondered.

Instead of waiting passively, she brought it up during her 1:1 with her manager.

"I've been thinking about what growth could look like here," Lia said. "I'm not looking to leave—I just want to explore how I can contribute in bigger ways."

Her manager appreciated the initiative. "That's great to hear. Have you documented any goals in your IDP recently?"

"I have," Lia said, pulling up her plan. "One area I'd love to explore is strategic planning or project leadership. I've noticed that's a strength I want to build on."

The conversation sparked momentum. Her manager helped her identify an upcoming internal initiative and connected her with a program manager who needed support. Over the next few weeks, Lia helped lead stakeholder updates, coordinate action items, and even facilitated a major milestone meeting.

A few months later, Lia's name came up in a talent calibration session.

"Who's that associate helping on the optimization project? She's making waves," a senior leader asked.

Lia's reputation, proactive mindset, and clearly defined goals had put her on the radar—without a title change. Eventually, Lia was tapped for a stretch assignment on the Corporate Strategy team. It wasn't a promotion—yet. But it was a stepping stone.

"I didn't wait for a new job title to start growing," Lia reflected. "I asked, aligned, and raised my hand. That made all the difference."

SEEING THE PATH AHEAD: A MOBILITY MAP

Lia's journey is a perfect example of internal mobility in action—but she's not alone. Many roles can act as springboards to new opportunities across departments within the same company. That's where a concept like the *Mobility Map* comes in.

A Mobility Map is a visual way to explore the possible directions your career could take within your company, based on the strengths and transferable skills you're developing today. It doesn't show a single "ladder," but a web of connected roles where your capabilities may already overlap 60–70%—you just haven't made the move yet.

Look at the example below (see **Figure 11.1**). Starting from *Business Operations Associate*, you can see how internal moves might unfold across departments like *Project Management, Marketing Operations,* or even *Corporate Strategy*. This is the professional equivalent of seeing what doors your current key might open—before you even ask for one to be unlocked.

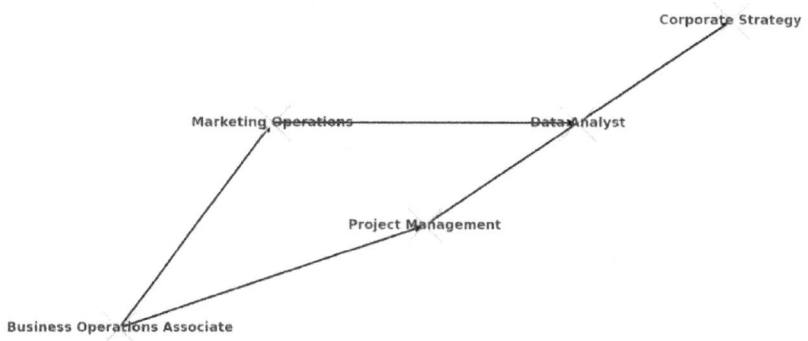

Table 11.1: Mobility Map: Sample Career Path starting from Business Operations

MY STORY

Opening Doors from the Inside

When I served as Head of Talent Development at Philips Semiconductors—a division of Philips Electronics—I had a front-row seat to how internal mobility and career progression really worked behind the scenes. One of our most powerful tools was the quarterly talent calibration meetings.

These sessions brought together global HR leaders and business executives to assess performance and potential using our leadership competency framework and a Performance/Potential Grid—Philips' version of the 9-box grid (see **Figure 11.2**).

While many associate these meetings strictly with promotion planning for top potentials in key roles across the company, we

245

also used it to spot early-career employees who showed real promise, particularly those within their first three to five years.

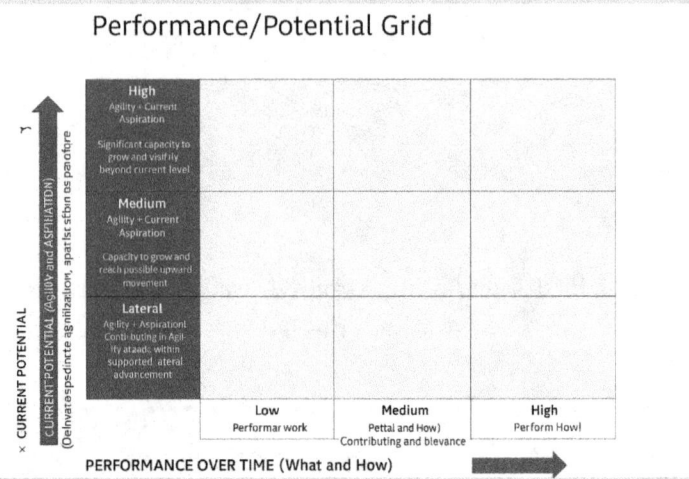

Figure 11.2: Philips' Performance & Potential Grid

What we saw was clear trend: internal movement was most dynamic at the early-career stage. These employees were more open to lateral shifts, cross-functional projects, and stretch assignments. They hadn't yet settled into rigid paths, which gave managers more flexibility to experiment and take risks— placing someone from Finance into a customer-facing project, or moving an operations associate into strategic planning. In many cases, these opportunities uncovered potential greater than what was visible on a performance review. You could say we were building mobility maps in real time, even if we didn't call it that.

Most of these assignments weren't formal promotions, but they were powerful developmental moves. They gave high-potential employees the chance to prove themselves in new environments, expand their networks, and gain visibility across the organization by trying out different career scenarios. Over time, a pattern emerged: those who embraced internal opportunities were the ones who grew into team leads, functional experts, and, eventually, executives in critical positions.

Another key ingredient was the shared belief in potential. When multiple leaders vouched for someone's readiness—even if that person didn't yet have the formal title—it created momentum. That informal consensus often sparked real opportunities: a stretch assignment, a temporary rotation, or an invitation to join a strategic initiative.

We didn't need a formal high-potential program to enable internal growth. What we needed was:

- A system to recognize potential early.
- Leaders willing to give people developmental opportunities.
- A culture that valued learning through doing.

Looking back, those talent calibration meetings weren't just about box placements. They were about possibilities—a lens through which we could see where talent might go next. They gave employees the opportunity to write their own mobility maps, one move at a time.

⚲AN INSIDER'S VIEW ⚲

HOW TALENT REALLY GETS NOTICED

The Internal mobility doesn't happen in a vacuum. Behind every promotion, transfer, or stretch assignment is a conversation—or several.

HR and leadership teams regularly conduct performance calibrations to assess and develop talent. These sessions draw from inputs like 9-box grids (which plot performance against potential), manager evaluations, peer feedback, and notes from career conversations. If you've been documenting your goals in your Individual Development Plan (IDP), seeking feedback, and showing initiative, you're more likely to be flagged as "ready for more."

But here's the kicker: these decisions aren't just about your output. They're about your *reputation*. Have you been dependable under pressure? Do others want to work with you? Are you proactive or reactive? Talent discussions often revolve around these very real, very human signals.

Mentors help guide and develop you. Champions push your name forward when it counts. To move up or across internally, both relationships matter—but champions, especially those with organizational influence, can make all the difference.

Companies embracing skills-first frameworks are also creating internal "mobility maps"—tools that identify transferable skills between roles. For example, a Business Operations Associate might have 70% of the competencies needed for a marketing operations role. If your company offers a talent marketplace or skills-matching tool, use it. If not, start building your own informal map: ask yourself, "*Where else could my current skills apply?*"

INTERNAL MOBILITY ACTION PLAN

Step	Action	Why It Matters
1. Clarify Goals	Use your IDP to identify areas of interest for internal growth.	Aligns career development with company direction.
2. Track Wins	Document your accomplishments quarterly.	Keeps you read for career conversations and visibility moments.
3. Stay Visible	Present updates, lead meetings, or contribute to cross-functional projects.	Builds your internal reputation and reach.
4. Seek Feedback	Get input from your manager, peers, and mentors.	Ensures you're known for being coachable and growth-oriented.
5. Build Relationships	Cultivate a mentor and a champion.	Champions advocate for your potential

		when you're not in the room.
6. Start the Conversation	Ask your manager how to prepare for internal roles.	Signals initiative and opens doors.

Table 11.3: Internal Mobility Action Plan Template

🐂 Let's Be Bullish:

Internal mobility is the professional version of the hidden ladder—it's not always advertised, but it exists. The key is knowing where it is and how to climb it (see **Table 11.3**).

Everything you've learned so far—delivering performance, clarifying your career goals through an IDP, understanding the 9-box, and navigating peer feedback—has set you up for this moment. Internal moves don't rely on wishful thinking. They rely on readiness, visibility, and trust.

If you want to grow within your company, ask yourself:

- Does my IDP reflect areas I want to explore?
- Have I earned a reputation for being reliable and resourceful?
- Do I have someone advocating for me?

These aren't just checkboxes. They're the signals that show leaders you're not just good where you are—you're ready for what's next.

And remember: great managers don't hoard talent—they help develop it. The best companies are learning that growing from within is not only cost-effective—it's strategic. They're not just filling jobs. They're building futures.

So ask the question. Raise your hand. Explore that open internal role. Be bullish about your growth.

BULLISH PRO TIPS

- **Know the ladder exists.** Internal mobility is real—but you have to seek it out, not wait for an invitation.

- **Track your wins visibly.** Make your value known across teams, not just within your current role.

- **Use performance reviews to explore growth.** Ask: "What's next for me here?" and "Where do you see potential?"

- **Build cross-functional relationships.** Visibility beyond your team can unlock hidden opportunities.

- **Ask HR or your manager about internal mobility programs.** Skills-first roles, talent marketplaces, or stretch assignments might be closer than you think.

Closing Reflection

Career mobility is about seeing opportunities before they're obvious. Yet even growth won't matter if your workplace doesn't make you feel valued.

Let's Recap!

- Internal mobility opens doors to promotions, lateral roles, and cross-functional experience

- Your performance, potential, and reputation all matter in talent discussions

- Champions and mentors play different roles—both are valuable

- Use your IDP, peer feedback, and documented wins to prepare

- Companies that grow talent internally win in agility, retention, and innovation

You don't need to leave to level up. Sometimes, the next step is just one ladder away—hidden, but well within reach.

12

CHAPTER

———

DO YOU FEEL VALUED?

I t's expected today that you won't stay with the same company for your entire career—those days are long gone. After a few years in the same role, it's natural to begin asking deeper questions about your path:

- *Am I truly valued here?*
- *Should I explore new opportunities?*
- *Is it time to test the job market?*

These thoughts often arise when you see peers moving on to new roles or receive compelling messages from recruiters. While the questions may sound tactical, they often reflect something deeper:

a desire for purpose, recognition, and connection to the work you do.

As you enter the 'Engagement & Separation' stage of the Employee Lifecycle, such considerations reflect a deep-seated need for validation and purpose in your work. Employees generally want to believe that their efforts matter and that their contributions make a meaningful difference at the company, regardless of their job title.

Encouragingly, the APA's 2024 Work in America survey offers a positive outlook. It reveals that many employees feel valued in their roles. Over 86% of respondents reported that their work positively impacts society, and 93% expressed pride in their achievements. Additionally, the percentage of employees intending to seek new jobs has slightly decreased, from 34% in 2022 to 29% in 2024. This trend indicates that many employees are finding satisfaction and purpose in their current positions, despite a changing job market.

THE UNSEEK SIGNALS

Building on this, when employees are genuinely happy and feel valued, several positive symptoms become evident.[42] One clear sign is increased engagement. Satisfied employees are more likely to actively take part in team discussions, contribute ideas, and volunteer for additional responsibilities. This enthusiasm and sense of ownership benefit both their personal growth and the company's success. Higher productivity and a willingness to exceed expectations often follow, illustrating the tangible benefits of feeling valued.

Positive emotional well-being is another indicator of job satisfaction. Employees who feel valued tend to be more resilient to workplace stress and keep a positive outlook on their work environment. They are less likely to experience burnout or disengagement and generally achieve a healthier work-life balance. This improved emotional state contributes to a supportive and cohesive workplace culture, enhancing overall job satisfaction.

A strong sense of recognition and accomplishment is also a significant sign of happiness at work. Employees who feel their contributions are acknowledged often display pride in their achievements. Constructive feedback motivates them to set and pursue personal and professional goals. This recognition not only boosts their morale but also fosters a sense of loyalty to the organization, promoting long-term retention and job satisfaction.

WHEN IT'S TIME TO EXPLORE

However, despite these positive signs, employees might consider exploring new opportunities for various reasons beyond personal dissatisfaction. Feelings of stagnation, lack of career advancement, or misalignment with organizational values can prompt such considerations. A strained relationship with a manager can also be a major factor. Meanwhile, the appeal of new challenges, higher compensation, or a more supportive work culture may prompt employees to consider whether the grass is truly greener elsewhere.[43] Deciding to leave isn't just about escaping dissatisfaction—it's about finding a role that aligns more closely with your evolving career goals.

THE ROI OF FEELING VALUED

Inspiring and motivating a team is not merely an aspiration for leaders; it is a fundamental strategic imperative. Research from the University of Oxford highlights this, revealing that employees who are happy and engaged are 13% more productive compared to their less satisfied counterparts. This productivity boost is crucial, as a motivated workforce directly affects organizational success and growth. In contrast, disengaged employees can cause significant economic damage, contributing to losses equivalent to 9% of global GDP—an alarming $8.8 trillion, as reported by Gallup. Such figures highlight the critical need for leaders to foster a positive work environment, as the cost of disengagement extends far beyond individual performance and affects the overall health of the organization.

When employees feel recognized and appreciated, they experience greater job satisfaction, creativity, and a willingness to take constructive risks. This sense of worth fosters a dynamic and innovative work environment. Conversely, feeling undervalued can lead to significant mental health challenges, including depression and anxiety.

THE NEW ERA OF ENGAGEMENT

In the post-pandemic era, characterized by trends such as "quiet quitting," where employees do the bare minimum, and "quiet vacationing," where they mentally check out despite being present, the necessity of feeling valued has become more pronounced than ever.[44] Workers are increasingly reassessing their work-life balance and seeking roles where they can make a meaningful impact. Achieving a sense of substantial contribution is challenging if an organization lacks a culture of respect and recognition. Companies that do not nurture such an environment may struggle to retain talent, as employees who feel undervalued are more likely to explore opportunities elsewhere.

Ultimately, your decision to remain with or leave a company depends on how well your role aligns with your personal values and career objectives. Organizations that build a culture of respect and appreciation not only retain their employees but also inspire them to perform at their best and innovate. For you, evaluating your job satisfaction and sense of value is important. Consider whether your current role supports your professional aspirations and contributes to your overall sense of fulfillment.

By taking the time to evaluate these aspects, you can make informed decisions that ensure your career is both rewarding and aligned with what truly matters to you.

OWEN'S STORY

When Doubt Creeps In

Owen worked as a Financial Analyst for a fintech company in Austin, Texas. Despite enjoying his job and working with a supportive team, he had recently been feeling increasingly uncertain about his future at the company. Friends had suggested he consider new opportunities, and recruiters had been reaching out with tempting offers. This growing sense of doubt led Owen to schedule a Zoom call with Kaley, his HR Business Partner.

As he logged into the video meeting, Owen noticed the sunlight streaming through his window, casting a warm glow across his workspace. Kaley appeared on the screen with a reassuring smile, ready to provide support.

"Thank you for meeting with me, Kaley," Owen said, his voice carrying a note of hesitation.

"Of course, Owen. What's on your mind?" Kaley asked, leaning forward slightly into her camera, her tone inviting and attentive.

Owen took a deep breath. "I've been with the company for almost three years now, and lately, I've been feeling restless. I keep wondering if I should start exploring new opportunities, but I can't quite figure out why I'm feeling this way."

Kaley nodded thoughtfully. "It sounds like you're at a crossroads. Can you tell me more about what's been contributing to these feelings?"

Owen hesitated, searching for the right words. "It's not that I dislike my job or my team. I actually value both. It's just— sometimes I wonder if what I'm doing really matters—or if anyone notices. Seeing colleagues move on to new roles and receiving messages from recruiters makes me wonder if I'm truly valued here."

Kaley's expression softened with empathy. "It's natural to question your role from time to time, especially when you're seeing changes around you. Are there specific events or patterns that might have triggered these feelings?"

Owen thought for a moment. "I've been feeling somewhat disconnected. Recent projects haven't felt as impactful as I hoped, and I haven't received much feedback from management. I sometimes wonder if my efforts are being recognized."

Kaley nodded in understanding. "It sounds like you might be experiencing a sense of stagnation or lack of acknowledgment. These feelings can often lead to questioning your place within the organization. Have you had a chance to discuss these concerns with your manager?"

Owen shook his head. "Not yet. I've been reluctant to bring it up, fearing it might seem like I'm complaining."

Kaley leaned in slightly, her tone supportive. "Addressing your concerns openly is important. Your manager might not be aware of your feelings, and having this conversation could provide clarity and lead to potential solutions. It could also help you assess if your current role aligns with your long-term career goals."

Owen appeared thoughtful. "That makes sense. I guess I've been afraid that if I raise these issues, it might be too late or that I'll be seen as dissatisfied."

Kaley smiled gently. "Discussing your concerns and seeking feedback isn't a sign of dissatisfaction; it's a proactive step toward personal and professional growth. If you're considering exploring new opportunities, reflect on what aspects of your job you find fulfilling and what might be missing. Understanding your core values and career goals can help clarify whether a change is necessary or if there are ways to rediscover purpose in your current role."

Owen's face brightened with relief. "Thank you, Kaley. I hadn't thought about it that way. I'll start by having an honest conversation with my manager and reflecting on my career goals."

Kaley gave him an encouraging nod through the screen. "That sounds like a great plan. Remember, aligning your work with your values is key. Whether you decide to stay or pursue new opportunities, ensuring that your role fulfills your professional and personal goals is essential."

As Owen ended the Zoom call, he felt a renewed sense of clarity. He realized that staying or leaving wasn't the only decision—rediscovering meaning in his current role was jus as important.

The conversation had provided Owen with valuable insights and a clearer direction for his career. Whether he chose to remain at the company or seek new opportunities, he now had a better understanding of his needs and how to address them.

The story of Owen's conversation with his HR Business Partner highlights several key lessons for employees navigating career uncertainty, which is quite normal. Firstly, open communication is essential. Owen's initial hesitation to discuss his concerns with his manager reflects a common fear of being perceived as discontented. However, the dialogue with Kaley demonstrates that expressing your feelings and seeking feedback can lead to significant clarity and potential solutions. Addressing issues proactively with your manager or HR is crucial for assessing whether your current role aligns with your career goals and for exploring potential avenues for improvement or growth.

Another vital lesson from Owen's experience is the importance of self-reflection. His restlessness and sense of disconnection reveal the need to evaluate your core values, job satisfaction, and career aspirations. Understanding what aspects of your work are fulfilling and identifying any gaps can guide you in making informed decisions about your career path.

This introspection helps you determine whether the challenges you face can be resolved within your current role or if pursuing new opportunities is the right step toward achieving personal and professional fulfillment.

SHOULD I STAY OR SHOULD I GO?

If you are contemplating leaving your current job, it's essential to clarify what is driving your decision. *Are you seeking higher compensation, a more prestigious job title, or a role with different responsibilities?* Identifying what you hope to gain from a new position can help you assess whether these factors are worth the potential risks and uncertainties of changing jobs. Sometimes, perceptions of stagnation, lack of career advancement, or misalignment with organizational values can prompt such considerations.

The allure of new challenges, better compensation, or a more supportive work culture can be enough to make even the most loyal employee reconsider their future. Therefore, ensure that any change aligns with your long-term goals and values, and evaluate whether it genuinely offers the enhancements you're seeking.

Before making the jump, do your homework on the external opportunities you're considering. Reach out to current or former employees through LinkedIn to gain insight into the company's culture and work environment. Look at company ratings on Glassdoor to understand employee satisfaction and any potential red flags. Exploring these avenues can provide a clearer picture of what to expect and help you make a more informed decision.

Remember, the grass is not always greener on the other side; new roles may come with their own set of challenges and compromises.

Lastly, seeking support and guidance from others can be empowering. The constructive feedback and empathetic listening Owen received from Kaley highlight the importance of leveraging external support in navigating career challenges. Remember, you're not alone in facing career dilemmas. Seeking guidance from mentors, colleagues, or HR professionals can be invaluable in gaining clarity and making well-informed decisions about your future, especially when external recruiters present enticing "sales pitches."

WHEN YOU FEEL VALUED

Valuing employees brings substantial benefits from a company perspective. Creating a healthy, engaging company culture directly affects productivity, processes, and profits. Organizations that focus on employee experience through targeted activities, initiatives, and incentives tend to see higher performance levels. Employees who feel appreciated and valued are not only more productive but also contribute positively to the company's overall success.[45]

However, only 61% of employees currently feel appreciated at work. Many companies rely on compensation as a primary means of keeping staff, but despite 80% of employers believing that employees leave for higher pay, only 12% actually do. Research shows that 79% of individuals who leave their jobs cite "lack of appreciation" as their primary reason for departure.

A less obvious but significant benefit of appreciating employees is the enhancement of open and honest communication within the organization. Valued employees are more likely to share valuable information with their managers in a non-judgmental manner, fostering a culture of transparency and collaboration. This positively influences the overall company culture.

When companies show respect for their employees, they cultivate an environment that supports continuous professional development, engagement, and long-term commitment. This approach leads to a healthier and more productive organization, where employees are motivated to stay and grow rather than seeking new opportunities due to dissatisfaction or a poor company culture.

Investing in employee engagement offers multifaceted rewards. Engaged employees demonstrate improved productivity, with research indicating that highly engaged staff can boost productivity by up to 20%. This increased productivity often translates into superior performance outcomes and provides a competitive market advantage.

When an organization prioritizes employee engagement, employees feel more motivated by, prideful of, and connected to both leaders and the company. Even small efforts to boost engagement can help reduce turnover and related costs. Replacing employees incurs substantial expenses, including recruitment, training, and lost productivity. Engaged employees are more likely to remain with the company, leading to up to 40% lower turnover rates in organizations with high engagement levels.

Employee engagement is just one facet of the employee experience, but it plays a significant role in shaping this experience. Engaged employees also enhance customer satisfaction. They are more likely to deliver excellent customer service, which in turn fosters customer loyalty and contributes to business growth. Moreover, engaged staff are more innovative and open to change, driving creativity and adaptability in a rapidly evolving market.

A positive company culture emerges from a focus on engagement. Employees who feel recognized and valued contribute to a supportive work environment, improving internal relations and enhancing the company's reputation as an employer of choice.[46] This positive reputation attracts top talent and strengthens organizational commitment.

Investing in employee well-being, including work-life balance and mental health support, reduces burnout and absenteeism, promoting a resilient workforce. The cumulative impact of these factors results in enhanced financial performance, with companies exhibiting higher profitability and achieving their financial targets.

THE ENGAGEMENT PULSE CHECK

To sustain high engagement levels, it is important to ask for regular feedback through surveys. These surveys provide insights into employees' perspectives, helping organizations understand their needs and identify areas for improvement. Acting on feedback not only shows commitment but also fosters a culture of continuous improvement and mutual respect.

Here are twelve essential questions that are commonly found in surveys to effectively gauge and enhance employee engagement:

1. On a scale of 1 to 10, how happy are you at work?
2. Would you refer someone to work here?
3. Do you have a clear understanding of your career or promotion path?
4. Do you feel valued in the workplace?

5. How often do you receive recognition from your manager or direct supervisor?

6. Did you receive recognition the last time you completed a big project or assignment?

7. Do you believe you'll be able to reach your full potential here?

8. Do you foresee yourself working here one year from now?

9. Do you believe the leadership team takes your feedback seriously?

10. What three words would you use to describe our culture?

11. Do you believe we live authentically by our organizational values?

12. Do you have fun at work?

Both employees and companies benefit from constructive criticism shared through engagement surveys. By acting on employee feedback, companies can make their staff feel valued, thereby enhancing engagement and fostering a positive outlook. This cycle of feedback and improvement is crucial for maintaining a motivated and satisfied workforce, contributing to the organization's success.

Improving employee engagement is an ongoing, dynamic process for many organizations, and there's no quick fix for sustained engagement. While some tips and tricks may provide short-term relief, a strategic approach is essential for long-term success.

Addressing identified engagement issues is just the beginning; maintaining these improvements is vital. Many companies adopt an employee feedback loop model to ensure their engagement initiatives have a lasting impact:

THE COLLECT-UNDERSTAND-ACT CYCLE

1. **Collect:** Design a survey with targeted questions to gather meaningful data.

2. **Understand:** Analyze the results to identify key drivers of engagement.

3. **Act:** Share the findings with your team, develop an action plan, and implement meaningful changes. This step is critical, as employees are more likely to respond positively to future surveys if they see their feedback leading to real action.

By following these 3-steps, companies can foster a culture of continuous improvement and genuine employee engagement. Consistently acting on employee feedback not only boosts morale but also drives overall organizational success. This proactive approach ensures that employees feel heard and valued, creating a positive and productive workplace environment.

Prioritizing employee engagement yields substantial benefits. An initiative-taking approach enhances innovation, productivity, well-being, and profit while reducing costly issues such as staff turnover, absenteeism, and inventory issues.

Every organization is unique, with distinct concerns, strengths, and priorities. What matters to your employees may differ from those in another company. To enhance engagement, measure and evaluate your current situation, then analyze and act to improve it.

The collect-understand-act cycle is a proven method for success, utilized by many companies. Identify factors impacting engagement, act on the findings, and continuously re-evaluate to refine your approach. Through persistent inquiry and action, you can effectively improve workforce engagement and boost your bottom line.

♈ Let's Be Bullish:

Even with the best intentions, disengagement can sneak up on you. But there are signs—if you know where to look.

Is it possible to predict when an employee is on their way out?

Many companies use employee engagement surveys and exit interviews to evaluate reasons for leaving patterns in the workforce.[47] However, there are few tools available for employees to perform a self-assessment to identify signs of disengagement.

Researchers at Harvard Business Review asked close to 100 managers how the behavior of their peers and subordinates shifted in the months prior to their voluntary departures. Additionally, researchers surveyed 100 employees to find out how their own behavior changed before they left voluntarily.[48] To help you assess your level of engagement and address any potential issues, we've created this self-assessment tool (see **Table 12.1**).

Take a moment to reflect on each indicator of disengagement listed below. Your honest responses will provide insights into areas where you may need improvement or support. By completing this worksheet, you will be better equipped to identify specific concerns and take proactive steps to enhance your job satisfaction.

Theme	Indicator	Yes/No
Frequent absences or tardiness	You may not prioritize your work responsibilities and may take unplanned absences, arrive late, or leave early without a care in the world.	
Leaving Work Earlier Than Usual	Regularly leaving work before the end of the day without a valid reason may indicate disengagement.	
Increased Absenteeism or Frequent Sick Days	A pattern of frequent sick days or extended absences can be a sign of deeper disengagement.	
Lack of Enthusiasm	Employees who are not engaged may seem unenthusiastic or uninterested in their work. This could mean they show minimal effort, are not keen on taking on additional responsibilities, or simply lack motivation.	

Decline in Quality of Work	A noticeable drop in the quality of work, including errors or incomplete tasks, can signal disengagement.	
Lower Work Productivity	A noticeable decline in the quantity of work produced can be a sign of disengagement.	
Resistance to Feedback	You may react defensively or show resistance to constructive criticism or feedback.	
Lack of Initiative	You may stop taking initiative, waiting for direction rather than proactively seeking ways to improve or contribute.	
Minimal Participation in Meetings	You may participate less actively in meetings, rarely contributing ideas or feedback.	
Acting Less Like a Team Player	Reduced participation in team activities or collaborative efforts can indicate disengagement.	
Avoiding Colleagues	Disengaged employees may distance themselves from their colleagues, avoiding team activities, discussions, or collaborations.	

Emotional Withdrawal	Exhibiting signs of emotional withdrawal, such as a lack of enthusiasm or engagement in casual conversations or social activities, can be an indicator.	
Negative Vibes	You may exhibit negative behaviors such as complaining, gossiping, or expressing dissatisfaction openly.	
Expressing Dissatisfaction with Manager	Open expressions of dissatisfaction or criticism directed towards management may reflect a lack of engagement.	
Expressing Dissatisfaction with Team Members	Negative comments or complaints about team members can be an indicator of disengagement.	
Expressing Dissatisfaction with Their Job	Ongoing complaints or a lack of enthusiasm about job responsibilities may signal disengagement.	
Low Commitment to the Company	You may not feel a sense of loyalty or commitment to their company.	
Changes in Appearance or Behavior	Significant changes in personal appearance or behavior, such as a decline in dressing professionally or	

	changes in demeanor, can be a sign of disengagement.	
Frequent Job Searching or Network Expansion	Actively seeking new job opportunities or expanding professional networks outside the company may indicate an intent to leave.	
Less Willing to Commit to Long-Term Timelines	Showing reluctance or hesitation to commit to long-term projects or deadlines may reflect disengagement.	
Less Focus on Job-Related Matters	Decreased attention to job responsibilities and priorities can be a sign of disengagement.	
A Negative Change in Attitude	Any significant shift towards a more negative or disinterested attitude in the workplace can be a sign of disengagement.	
Lack of Career Advancement	Feeling stuck in your current role with little to no opportunities for growth or promotion can lead to disengagement. If you believe your career is not progressing, it may impact your overall motivation and commitment.	

Not Satisfied with Compensation	Dissatisfaction with your salary or benefits package can contribute to feelings of disengagement. If you feel that your compensation does not reflect your efforts and contributions, it might lead to decreased motivation and performance.	

Table 12.1: Disengagement Assessment Tool

If you relate to any of these signs and have marked "yes" on several disengagement themes, addressing these concerns proactively is crucial for improving your job satisfaction. Begin by taking an objective stance and assessing the dynamics of your relationship with your manager and your overall role within the company. Identify specific factors contributing to conflicts or a lack of motivation.

If issues like limited growth potential persist, initiate a conversation with a trusted individual at your company. Reflect on your ideal position and how it aligns with your career goals.

To guide you through this process, here's a helpful outline:

REIGNITE YOUR ENGAGEMENT – 10 STEPS

1. **Schedule a Discussion with Your Manager, Colleagues or HR Business Partner:**

   o **Action:** Request a one-on-one meeting with a trusted individual you can confide in to discuss your self-assessment results.

273

○ **Purpose:** This conversation will help you share your concerns, gain insights, and collaboratively identify potential solutions.

2. **Reflect on Your Job Fit and Responsibilities:**

   ○ **Action:** Evaluate whether your current role aligns with your skills, interests, and career goals.

   ○ **Purpose:** Consider whether adjustments to your responsibilities or exploring a different role within the company might better fit your strengths.

3. **Seek Support and Resources:**

   ○ **Action:** Take full advantage of available resources, such as professional development programs, counseling services, and mentorship opportunities.

   ○ **Purpose:** These resources can provide the support needed to address challenges and enhance your job satisfaction.

4. **Enhance Communication:**

   ○ **Action:** Engage in open, honest discussions with your manager and colleagues about your job satisfaction and any issues you're facing.

   ○ **Purpose:** Regular feedback and communication can help resolve concerns and improve your work experience.

5. **Assess the Work Environment and Culture:**

    o **Action:** Reflect on the work environment and company culture to identify factors contributing to your disengagement.

    o **Purpose:** Addressing these factors can help create a more positive and supportive workplace.

6. **Set Clear Goals and Expectations:**

    o **Action:** Collaborate with your manager to establish clear, achievable goals and expectations for your role.

    o **Purpose:** Clear goals provide direction and motivation, helping you feel more focused and engaged.

7. **Recognize Your Achievements:**

    o **Action:** Track your accomplishments and seek recognition for your contributions.

    o **Purpose:** Recognizing and celebrating your achievements can boost morale and reinforce your sense of value.

8. **Explore Growth Opportunities:**

    o **Action:** Investigate opportunities for professional growth, such as training programs or new projects.

- **Purpose:** Engaging in growth opportunities can reignite your interest and open new avenues for advancement.

9. **Consider a Role Change:**

    - **Action:** Discuss the possibility of transitioning to a different role or department that better aligns with your interests and strengths.
    - **Purpose:** A role change can offer a fresh perspective and renewed enthusiasm.

10. **Monitor and Reflect Regularly:**

    - **Action:** Continuously assess your engagement levels and reflect on your progress.
    - **Purpose:** Ongoing reflection helps you stay aware of your engagement and make necessary adjustments.

Taking proactive steps to address disengagement can significantly improve your job satisfaction and overall work experience. Identifying the root causes of your dissatisfaction and seeking support to resolve them is crucial while you are still at your present work.

Before deciding to resign, fully utilize the internal resources and support available within the organization. Engage in professional development opportunities, seek guidance from mentors or counselors, and have open, honest discussions with your manager about your concerns and career goals.

WHEN THE CULTURE IS THE PROBLEM

However, if the primary reason for wanting to leave your job is due to a toxic work culture, it's important to take action. Let's take a minute to elaborate on what this means.

A toxic work environment, simply put, sucks! It is unpleasant or harmful to employees and can take many forms, including bullying, harassment, unethical behavior, and dishonesty. And, of course, toxicity is not limited to face-to-face interactions; remote workers can also experience harassment through email, video calls, and chat applications.

A toxic workplace can also be one that offers inadequate compensation, fails to recognize or reward outstanding achievements, prioritizes customers over employees, restricts internal movement, denies employees a voice, breaches trust, or demands continuous work without allowing for adequate rest. Regardless of the situation, it's important to address these issues. Your company should have a confidential process for reporting and handling such serious matters, often referred to as a whistleblower policy. This policy ensures that employees can safely report unethical behavior or workplace misconduct without fear of retaliation.

If your reasons for leaving are more personal or professional in nature, you may be pleasantly surprised by the positive outcomes that can result from these conversations with your manager. If the organization values you and recognizes your potential through tools like a 9-box grid, it may implement various retention strategies to address your concerns and enrich your work experience. These strategies could include offering new growth opportunities, adjusting your responsibilities, providing additional training, or exploring other roles within the company.

While turnover is a natural part of any business, proactive measures can help reduce its frequency. Addressing your issues early and exploring all available support can lead to meaningful improvements and rekindle your enthusiasm for your role. Remember, your well-being and job satisfaction are crucial.

The company has invested in your career; giving them a chance to address your concerns before resigning would be ideal. You may be pleased to find that your manager or HR Business Partner asks, *"What would I need to do to keep you?"* Collaborating with your manager to enhance your work life can lead to a more fulfilling career and help you make a more informed decision about your future with the company.

From my experience as a Human Resources Executive, I've observed many employees hesitate to discuss their concerns with managers, fearing rejection or being labeled as "entitled," and instead choose to seek employment elsewhere. However, ambitious employees who are determined to advance their careers do not shy away from articulating their goals and setting clear expectations for their employers.

This approach is not about entitlement but about forging a clear path for career development and leadership, continuing to produce and progress, and accelerating their professional journey. If you decide to stay with your current employer and work through your concerns, bravo! This choice can lead to a success story worth celebrating and showcase your resilience and commitment. However, if the signs suggest that something might be wrong—whether with you or your work—it's crucial to address the issue head-on.

If the problem is with you, don't wait for miracles to happen. Take a deep breath and seek professional support—perhaps you're just tired, need to boost your self-esteem, or need to establish boundaries with colleagues or your manager. Proactive steps to improve your well-being can significantly enhance your job satisfaction and performance. In other words, take care of yourself!

On the other hand, if the problem lies with your work and change seems improbable, it's time to consider finding another job. If, like Owen after several years of service, you determine that you've exhausted all opportunities and it's time to move on, that's a valid and respectable decision.

HOW TO LEAVE WITHOUT BURING BRIDGES

Once you've decided it's time to leave, notifying your manager of your resignation can be challenging, especially if you fear conflict. It's crucial to approach the conversation with clarity and respect. Even if you are confident in your decision to move on from your first job after graduation, having an open and honest discussion about your departure helps to close this chapter constructively. This not only fosters a positive final impression but also ensures you avoid burning bridges, preserving valuable professional relationships for the future.

Ultimately, your career path should align with your personal and professional goals. Whether you stay or leave, aim to exit on positive terms, as how you leave is often as significant as how you arrived. Professional connections may resurface, and maintaining a positive final impression can open doors for future opportunities.

BULLISH PRO TIPS

- **Assess your satisfaction.** If you're starting to question your value, listen to that voice—then act.

- **Look for signals.** Lack of recognition, unclear growth paths, and poor manager relationships are red flags.

- **Start internal first.** Before you browse LinkedIn, ask: "Have I explored every growth opportunity here?"

- **Don't stay silent.** If you're feeling overlooked, speak with your manager—don't let frustration fester.

- **Know your worth.** Your impact matters. If you're not valued where you are, go where you will be.

Closing Reflection

Engagement fuels performance, while disengagement can quietly pull you away. At some point, you may face the decision: do you stay, or is it time to go?

Let's Recap!

- **Evaluate Your Value:** Reflect on your contributions and how they align with the company's goals. Consider seeking feedback from colleagues and management to gauge how your efforts are perceived and whether you feel truly valued.

- **Explore Opportunities:** Assess if your current role meets your career aspirations and job satisfaction. If there are significant gaps or unmet needs, explore other opportunities within or outside the company that may better align with your career goals and personal growth.

- **Boosts Retention and Performance:** Companies that prioritize employee engagement create a culture of respect and appreciation, which helps retain talent and motivates employees to perform at their best, leading to higher productivity and quality of work.

- **Enhances Organizational Success:** Companies invest time and energy to have engaged employees as they are more committed and aligned with the company's goals, driving overall organizational success through improved performance and achievement of strategic objectives.

- **Strengthens Company Culture:** A focus on engagement helps build a positive company culture, characterized by trust, collaboration, and mutual respect, which strengthens team cohesion and workplace morale.

- **Identify and Address Issues:** Take proactive steps to identify the root causes of disengagement, such as lack of motivation or dissatisfaction with responsibilities, and work to address these issues to enhance your overall job satisfaction.

- **Utilize Available Resources:** Engage with company resources, such as professional development programs, mentorship, and open communication with management, to resolve concerns and improve your work experience.

Ultimately, recognizing your worth—and taking proactive steps when you don't feel it—is essential to owning your professional journey.

13

CHAPTER

———

WHEN IT'S TIME TO GO

At some point in your early career, you'll leave your first role. If you've spent a few years in the industry and are celebrating your third work anniversary, that moment might be now. Resigning and moving on is a significant milestone—it marks your transition from a "recent graduate" to a true "early-career professional."

This is an exciting time as you prepare to set out on a new chapter in your professional journey, possibly at your second company since graduation. Embrace this moment of growth and the new opportunities that lie ahead.

BEFORE YOU LEAVE

Before you begin your new job, it's customary to provide notice before your final day with the company. Depending on the country and workplace norms, this notice period can range from two weeks to a full month. During this transition, take time to reflect on your journey and how you've experienced each stage of the Employee Lifecycle:

Stage 1: Attraction & Recruitment:

This was when you discovered job opportunities, navigated the application process, and landed your role. The excitement of receiving an offer and the promise of new beginnings set the foundation for your career.

Stage 2: Onboarding & Assimilation:

This stage involved learning the ropes, understanding the company culture, and integrating into your team. You attended training sessions, met colleagues, and built initial competence and confidence.

Stage 3: Performance & Development:

Here, you honed your skills, took on new responsibilities, and worked towards your professional goals. Performance reviews, goal-setting sessions, and continuous learning opportunities marked this phase.

Stage 4: Total Rewards & Retention:

During this phase, you likely received performance reviews, salary adjustments, and promotions. Understanding how merit was determined and ensuring fair and competitive compensation became key aspects.

Stage 5: Engagement & Separation:

As you prepare to leave your role, assess your accomplishments and experiences. Engage in exit interviews, transition responsibilities, and prepare mentally and emotionally for your next endeavor.

ASHLEY'S STORY

Too Late to Stay

Over the years, I've built great teams and witnessed top talent move on to new opportunities. However, nothing quite prepared me for the day one of my top employees on the recruitment team, Ashley, decided to resign and join a competitor. The news struck me hard, and I felt an immediate wave of panic.

Ashley had been with the company for three years, consistently delivering outstanding results, and she was a favorite among her managers. Beyond her impressive performance, she was someone I had personally mentored and invested significant time in developing. Losing her felt like a personal and professional blow.

One Monday morning, Ashley scheduled a meeting with me. I could sense that something was off, but I wasn't prepared for the news she was about to deliver.

"Ashley, come in," I said, trying to sound as welcoming as possible despite the anxiety twisting in my stomach.

285

Ashley took a seat, her demeanor unusually solemn. "I've really enjoyed working here, but I've been offered a new position at a competitor, and I've decided to accept it."

My heart sank. "Ashley, I'm really sorry to hear that. You're a vital part of our team. Can I ask what prompted this decision?" Naturally, I went into action mode, thinking to myself, *I can fix this and turn it around.*

"It's not just one thing," she replied. "I've been feeling somewhat stagnant in my role here. The new job offers more growth opportunities and aligns better with my long-term career goals."

I took a deep breath, considering my next words carefully. "I understand how much this opportunity means to you. I don't want to lose you. Let's talk about this." I then blurted, *"What can I do so that you stay?"*

Ashley's gaze shifted down before meeting mine again. "I appreciate that, Ed, but it's not about the money or any immediate changes. I've already mentally prepared myself for this new challenge. It's time for me to move on."

The truth hit me with full force. Despite all the effort I had put into her development and the significant investment of time, **Ashley had already emotionally and mentally checked out.** It was most likely too late to change her mind.

"Ashley, I wasn't expecting this," I said, trying to mask my disappointment. "I've always believed in your potential and tried to provide opportunities for growth. What could I have done differently to prevent this?" I wasn't sure why I asked this; I guess I just wanted her to keep talking and maybe, just maybe, change her mind.

She sighed. "Ed, you've been a great mentor, and I appreciate everything you've done. But sometimes, it's about finding a new environment where I can grow in different ways. It's not a reflection on you or the team." I could tell her response was carefully considered.

I pondered silently, thinking about the effectiveness of a counteroffer. The conversation made it clear: proactive career development, regular employee satisfaction check-ins, and fostering a culture of growth are crucial.

After some awkward silence, I sensed Ashley was ready to wrap up. "Thank you for everything you've done here, Ashley. We're really going to miss you," I said sincerely. "Let's work to ensure your transition is as smooth as possible. Remember, you'll always have a place here if you decide to return."

"Thank you, Ed," Ashley replied, standing up. "I really appreciate your understanding and support."

As Ashley left my office, I reflected on a critical lesson: addressing the underlying issues that drive employees to leave is essential. When managers invest deeply in their team members and they choose to move on, it can be difficult to accept. Yet the best approach is often to let them go with professionalism and grace. This experience reshaped my approach to managing and retaining talent.

Ashley's exit reminded me that relationships outlast roles. Even after more than six years, I still stay in touch with her. Sometimes we exchange a quick hello, and other times she reaches out to share an update or ask for advice. I'm grateful that the foundation we built—rooted in trust and mutual respect—has allowed our relationship to continue long after her departure. That, to me, is the true measure of meaningful leadership and mentorship.

BRINGING THE BOOK FULL CIRCLE

As you step into your new role, draw on the lessons and tools covered in the previous chapters of this book. You may encounter many of the same challenges, and the strategies discussed earlier will remain relevant. The insights gained from your experiences, coupled with the knowledge acquired from this book, will be invaluable as you transition to your next position.

As the cycle begins all over again, you'll have the opportunity to build on your experiences, grow further, refine your craft, and continue advancing in your career. Each new cycle or expanded role brings fresh challenges and opportunities, allowing you to apply your accumulated wisdom, acquire new skills, and achieve even greater success.

Embrace this moment and use it as a steppingstone to greater success and fulfillment. The Employee Lifecycle is a continuous journey of growth, learning, and adaptation. By understanding and navigating each stage effectively, you set yourself up for long-term success.

As you move forward, remember that every ending is a new beginning, and each phase of your career brings new opportunities to achieve your goals and aspirations. Stay open to learning, remain adaptable, and keep striving for excellence, and you will continue to thrive in your professional journey.

EVOLUTION TO EARLY-CAREER PROFESSIONALS

As you move on to your new job opportunity, it's good practice to look back and see how much you have grown and developed since graduating from college. The transition from being a recent college graduate with zero years of experience to an early-career professional with three years of industry experience marks a significant evolution.

As a recent graduate, you entered the workforce full of enthusiasm and curiosity—ready to tackle the world. Armed with theoretical knowledge, some internship experience, and a degree, you brought a strong academic background, fresh perspectives, and high enthusiasm.

However, you may have lacked extensive practical experience, industry-specific skills, and a nuanced understanding of workplace dynamics. Eager to learn, adapt, and prove your capabilities, you possessed essential qualities for any newcomer. Now, let's look back and remember where you began:

Early Career Challenges:

Upon graduation, your initial phase in the workforce involved a steep learning curve. For instance, you might have faced the challenge of leading a project for the first time, where balancing multiple priorities and learning effective communication with different team members were key hurdles. Your focus was on absorbing as much knowledge as possible, asking questions, and seeking feedback.

During this period, you were likely introduced to the realities of day-to-day operations, where theoretical concepts had to be applied in practical scenarios. The enthusiasm and fresh perspectives you brought to the table were invaluable, but you needed guidance and mentorship to navigate complex tasks and understand industry-specific nuances.

As you moved through this initial phase, adapting to the pace and demands of your new role involved significant challenges. You might have struggled to manage tight deadlines or understand the intricacies of office politics. Your efforts to improve your time management and organizational skills were important during this period. Learning to balance these responsibilities while understanding the organizational culture requires resilience and a willingness to step out of your comfort zone. This phase was marked by a blend of excitement and challenges as you strived to bridge the gap between academic learning and professional application.

Transition to an Early-Career Professional:

Transitioning into an early-career professional with three years of industry experience brings a significant change in your attributes. For example, you now handle complex projects with greater ease. You may have successfully led a cross-departmental team to streamline a process, demonstrating both your leadership skills and ability to apply industry knowledge.

Your practical, hands-on experience has given you a deeper understanding of industry-specific practices and a more refined skill set. Your familiarity with workplace dynamics, ability to handle responsibilities, and established professional relationships now distinguish you from a recent graduate.

With three years of experience, your professional competence has significantly strengthened. You've developed problem-solving skills and resilience through various challenges, such as implementing advanced data analytics for strategic decisions.

The relationships you've built within the industry have become valuable assets, providing a network of contacts and resources that a recent graduate might not have. This network can open doors to new opportunities and collaborations, further advancing your career.

Career Growth and Stability:

In addition to these enhanced attributes, your experience now qualifies you for more senior roles with higher compensation. For instance, you may now be eligible for positions such as project manager or team lead. Your proven track record of handling complex projects and driving results has made you a strong candidate for these advanced roles. Employers value the practical experience and industry knowledge you bring to the table, and this increased value is often reflected in more senior job titles and higher compensation.

Importantly, this growth and achievement might not have been possible if you had frequently switched jobs and been labeled as a "job hopper" (see Chapter 2). Staying with one company through these critical early years allowed you to accumulate the experience, build relationships, and gain the credibility needed to advance in your career.

Frequent job changes can often prevent you from fully developing the skills and knowledge necessary for significant professional growth. By sticking with one organization, you demonstrated commitment, resilience, and the ability to overcome challenges—qualities highly valued by employers and crucial for long-term success.

Contributions and Leadership:

In contrast to the fresh perspectives of a recent graduate, you now bring a balanced view to your role. Your decisions are informed by both theoretical knowledge and practical experience. You might mentor new graduates, guiding them through the initial phases of their careers just as you were guided. Your contributions are not only recognized but also sought after, as you have proven your ability to deliver tangible results.

The confidence and credibility you've built over these years empower you to take on more complex and impactful projects, positioning you as a valuable asset to any organization.

This transition reflects a shift from learning and adaptation to mastery and innovation. As a seasoned, experienced professional, you have a full understanding of your area of specialization. You can resolve a wide range of issues in creative ways, leveraging both your experience and industry knowledge. This job is now a fully qualified, career-oriented, mid-level position, where you are not just performing tasks but also contributing to strategic goals and long-term success.

Reflecting on this evolution, the difference three years can make in one's career is profound. The initial enthusiasm and eagerness of a recent graduate are transformed into the seasoned expertise and strategic thinking of an early-career professional. Your journey has been marked by continuous learning, growth, and adaptation, each phase building on the previous one. You have moved from being guided to becoming a guide, from learning the ropes to mastering them, and from contributing to driving innovation and change.

🐂 Let's Be Bullish:

The transition from a new college graduate to an early-career professional is marked by significant growth and development; it likely happened in the blink of an eye. As you progress from the initial phase characterized by enthusiasm, fresh perspectives, and theoretical knowledge, you swiftly evolve into a seasoned professional with practical experience, industry-specific skills, and professional confidence.

This evolution, typically occurring over a span of about three years, prepares you for more senior roles and higher compensation, reflecting the increased value you bring to employers.

To help you assess how this rapid transformation applies to you at this stage of your career, the following comparison outlines the key differences between a 'new college graduate' and an 'early-career professional.'

Review these points to determine where you currently stand and to better understand the milestones you've achieved or areas for further development in your professional journey.

CONTRASTING TWO CAREER STAGES

To help you see your progress clearly, here's a side-by-side comparison of where you started and where you likely are now:

New College Graduate (0 Years Experience):

Strong Theoretical Knowledge:

Well-versed in core concepts and principles of their field through an earned college degree. Proficient in research methodologies and up to date on recent advancements.

Key Difference: Focused on learning theoretical frameworks without extensive practical application.

Eager to Learn:

Highly motivated and adaptable. Excellent problem-solving skills and open to feedback. Typically receives detailed instructions on all work.

Key Difference: Requires close supervision and detailed guidance to complete tasks effectively.

Limited Practical Experience:

May have internship or volunteer experience. Requires guidance and mentorship with a learning curve for applying theoretical knowledge to real-world scenarios. *Key Difference:* Less familiarity with industry-specific tools and processes.

Professional Skills:

Basic proficiency in industry-standard tools and software. Developing communication skills and learning to work within a team.

Key Difference: Limited practical skills and experience in applying them.

Career Focus:

Emphasis on learning and gaining initial work experience. Building a resume and exploring career interests. Seeking entry-level roles to start their career path.

Key Difference: Primary focus on learning and gaining experience.

Networking:

Initial networking through academic connections, internships, and career fairs. Building relationships with peers and mentors.

Key Difference: Early stages of building a professional network with less established connections.

Salary Expectations:

Entry-level compensation with growth potential. Compensation typically lower, reflecting limited experience.

Key Difference: Starting salary range with room for growth as experience increases.

Workplace Dynamics:

Learning to navigate office culture and workplace norms, ways of working. Understanding professional etiquette and organizational structure.

Key Difference: New to workplace dynamics and requires adaptation to organizational culture.

Next Steps

Focus on securing your entry-level position. Begin to build practical skills. Develop strong communication and soft skills. Ask questions and be curious, soak in as much knowledge as possible from others.

Early-Career Professional (3 Years Experience):

Applying Theoretical Knowledge:

Translating academic knowledge into practical solutions. Demonstrated ability to learn and adapt to new technologies and processes. Strong analytical and critical thinking skills. Hired for industry knowledge, skills, and experience.

Key Difference: Applies theoretical knowledge effectively in practical, real-world situations.

Building a Professional Network:

Developed relationships with colleagues, mentors, and industry professionals. Proficient in communication and collaboration skills. Able to leverage network for career advancement. Receives little instruction on day-to-day work, general instructions on new assignments.

Key Difference: Networked relationships provide career opportunities and support.

Proven Track Record:

Achieved measurable results in current role. Strong work ethic and ability to meet deadlines. Experience in project management or team leadership.

Key Difference: Demonstrated success and reliability in a professional setting.

Professional Skills:

Advanced proficiency in industry-standard tools and software. Strong communication, project management, and leadership skills. Capable of handling complex tasks and leading projects.

Key Difference: Highly developed practical skills with significant on-the-job experience.

Career Focus:

Considering career advancement opportunities and specialized roles. Focus on building expertise and taking on leadership responsibilities. Evaluating options for long-term career goals and growth.

Key Difference: Moving beyond entry-level roles to explore higher positions and specializations.

Networking:

Established a robust professional network with influential contacts. Actively seeks mentorship and sponsorship for career growth.

Key Difference: Well-connected network that provides substantial career support and opportunities.

Salary Expectations:

Higher compensation reflecting experience and proven performance. Eligible for more senior roles with increased responsibility and pay.

Key Difference: Higher salary range due to accumulated experience and skillset.

Workplace Dynamics:

Experienced in navigating office culture and contributing to team dynamics. Comfortable with professional etiquette and organizational structure.

Key Difference: Well-versed in workplace dynamics and effectively contributes to organizational goals.

Next Steps:

Consider pursuing advanced certifications or training to specialize within your field. Explore opportunities for career advancement within the current company. Develop leadership skills and take on more responsibility in projects. Continue networking and building relationships with mentors.

The progression from a new college graduate to an early-career professional illustrates a significant transformation in one's career journey in the blink of an eye. While new graduates bring strong theoretical knowledge and enthusiasm, they must focus on gaining practical experience and understanding workplace dynamics.

In contrast, early-career professionals leverage their experience to apply their knowledge practically, build extensive professional networks, and demonstrate a proven track record of achievements. Over time, this evolution not only enhances their skills and industry expertise but also positions them for more advanced roles and higher compensation. This journey highlights the importance of continual learning, professional growth, and strategic career planning in achieving long-term success.

BULLISH PRO TIPS

- **Resign professionally.** Give proper notice, tie up loose ends, and leave with grace—even if it's emotional.

- **Use your voice on the way out.** Your exit interview is a chance to offer thoughtful feedback—use it wisely.

- **Be remembered well.** Your last few weeks will shape people's lasting impression of you. Finish strong.

- **Don't burn bridges.** You never know when a former coworker or boss will cross your path again.

- **Keep doors open.** Even if you're ready to move on, stay open to being a Boomerang Employee someday.

- **Reputation follows up.** Your final impression will travel farther than you think.

Closing Reflection

Leaving your first role is more than an ending—it's a defining milestone. What follows is how you carry your reputation and relationships forward.

Let's Recap!

- **Milestone Transition**: Reaching your third work anniversary signifies the transition from a recent graduate to an early-career professional, marking a significant growth phase in your career.

- **Employee Lifecycle Reflection**: As you leave your current role, reflect on your progression through the Employee Lifecycle stages: Attraction & Recruitment, Onboarding & Assimilation, Performance & Development, Total Rewards & Retention, and Engagement & Separation.

- **Skill Evolution**: Over three years, you've moved from theoretical knowledge and initial challenges to practical expertise and leadership, enhancing your industry-specific skills and confidence.

- **Career Growth**: Staying with one organization has helped you build experience, relationships, and credibility, qualifying you for more senior roles and higher compensation.

- **Future Preparation**: Use the insights from your experiences and this book to embrace new opportunities, continue learning, and advance in your career as you begin a new role.

14

CHAPTER

RELATIONSHIPS MATTER

So, you've decided to voluntarily move on and resign from your company. As you prepare to leave your company, the relationships you've built—those who mentored you, challenged you, and supported your growth—become increasingly valuable. These are more than names on LinkedIn; they are assets for your future.

The connections you've developed over the years are more than just part of your professional network—they are pivotal assets that can significantly impact your future success. Transitioning to a new company offers a fresh start and exciting opportunities, but it also involves navigating new relationships while continuing to value and nurture those from your previous role.

In this chapter, we will delve into the key relationships that supported you during your tenure at your first job and explore why maintaining and fostering these connections is essential as you move forward (see **Table 14.1**). Although the specifics may vary from company to company and your experience is unique, understanding and leveraging these relationships can provide invaluable support, insights, and opportunities. By doing so, you will ensure a smoother transition and lay a strong foundation for your continued career growth.

KEY RELATIONSHIPS TO MAINTAIN
1. Your Manager
2. HR Business Partner
3. Mentor(s)
4. Colleagues
5. Executive Leadership
6. CEO
7. Clients or Customers
8. Industry Partners
9. Professional Associates or Networks
10. Personal Contacts

Table 14.1 Key Relationships to Maintain

1. **Your Manager**: Your manager has been a central figure in your professional development, providing guidance, feedback, and support. As you move to a new job,

maintaining a positive relationship with your previous manager can be beneficial. They can serve as a valuable reference, offer insights into your strengths and areas for improvement, and potentially provide networking opportunities within their professional circle.

2. **HR Business Partner**: Your HR Business Partner may have played an instrumental role in handling various administrative aspects of your employment and providing guidance, including performance reviews, conflict resolutions, and career development discussions. They can offer insights into company culture, your achievements, and areas of growth. A strong relationship with HR in your network as an ongoing resource can be useful for you. Additionally, they might be able to connect you with other professionals in your industry.

3. **Mentor(s)**: A mentor may have provided personalized guidance, advice, and encouragement, helping you navigate your career path and develop professionally. This relationship is invaluable, as mentors bring a wealth of experience and perspective. As you transition to a new role, maintaining contact with your mentor can offer ongoing support and strategic advice. They can assist you in evaluating new opportunities, provide insights into industry trends, and continue to support your growth and development.

4. **Colleagues**: Your colleagues may have been your day-to-day support network, collaborating on projects, sharing

knowledge, and offering camaraderie. These relationships are important for maintaining a positive work environment and fostering teamwork. Even as you move on, staying connected with your colleagues can offer ongoing professional support and open doors to future collaborations. They can also provide a sense of continuity and stability as you adjust to your new role.

5. **Executive Leadership**: Relationships with executives may have provided strategic insights and broaden your understanding of the company's direction and goals. These connections are often built through involvement in high-impact projects or initiatives. As you transition to a new company, maintaining relationships with executives from your previous role can be valuable. They can offer high-level advice, support, and potentially introduce you to influential contacts within your industry.

6. **CEO**: The CEO, as the top executive, represents the overall vision and strategy of the company. While direct interactions with the CEO might be less frequent, having had exposure to their leadership style and strategic priorities can be insightful. If you had the opportunity to work closely with the CEO, keeping this relationship positive and professional can be advantageous. They can offer broad industry perspectives and connections that may benefit your career.

7. **Clients or Customers**: If your role involved direct interactions with clients or customers, these relationships

are important to maintain. Positive client relationships can lead to future business opportunities and professional referrals. As you move to a new role, staying in touch with former clients can help you build a strong professional reputation and potentially lead to new opportunities.

8. **Industry Peers**: Connections with peers from industry events, conferences, or professional associations are valuable for staying informed about industry trends and opportunities. These relationships can provide support, collaboration, and knowledge sharing. As you transition to a new company, keeping in touch with industry peers can offer insights into best practices and trends, and they might also provide referrals or recommendations.

9. **Professional Associations or Networks**: Your involvement in professional associations or networks can offer ongoing support and opportunities for career advancement. These organizations often provide resources, events, and connections that are beneficial as you progress in your career. Maintaining relationships within these networks can help you stay engaged with industry developments and provide a platform for continued professional growth.

10. **Personal Contacts**: Sometimes, personal relationships with individuals who are knowledgeable about your industry or career can offer valuable support. These contacts might include former professors, advisors, or friends with industry experience. As you transition to a

new role, these personal connections can provide advice, referrals, and encouragement, helping you navigate your new professional landscape.

As you move on to new roles and opportunities, remember that the professional world is often smaller than it seems. Your paths may cross again with former colleagues, mentors, or managers in unexpected ways. Whether through networking events, industry conferences, or future collaborations, the professional relationships you've cultivated during your initial job will remain a vital part of your career journey.

These connections provide valuable industry insights, uncover new job opportunities, and strengthen your network of colleagues and mentors. Building and maintaining these relationships requires deliberate effort and attention. Investing time and energy into nurturing these connections will pay off, enhancing your career growth and opening doors to future opportunities. It's easier to form connections early in your career when you are recognized as a talented individual.

A key element to understand is the distinction between reputation and personal branding. According to Harvard Business Review, "Your reputation is made up of the opinions and beliefs people form about you based on your collective actions and behaviors." In contrast, personal branding is intentional and designed to differentiate you from the competition, establishing you as a thought leader in your industry.

In today's competitive job market, having a strong personal brand is essential.[49] It's not enough to be a proficient worker; you need to be noticed and remembered for your unique value.

Maintaining a positive reputation and a standout personal brand starts now; in fact, it began on day 'zero' with your company. The relationships you build, the reputation you foster, and the brand you create will follow you throughout your career.

As you continue to advance professionally, these elements will play a critical role in your success. They will influence how others perceive you, open new opportunities, and ensure that you are recognized as a valuable professional. By actively nurturing your professional network and investing in your personal brand, you lay the groundwork for ongoing growth and achievement.

So, as you transition into new roles, focus on strengthening your connections, maintaining a positive reputation, and building a compelling personal brand. These efforts will not only support your current career but will also pave the way for future successes and opportunities.

SUSAN'S STORY

When Honesty Gets Tricky

One afternoon, as I was wrapping up for the day, I received a call from an unfamiliar number. Curiosity got the better of me, so I answered.

"Hello, this is Ali from *Yellow Brick Road Staffing*. Is this Ed?"

"Yes, this is Ed. How can I help you?"

"Hi Ed, I'm currently considering a candidate for a role at one of our client companies as a 'senior recruiter'. I was hoping you could provide some insight into her professional skills and capabilities. Her name is Susan Roberts, and she mentioned you during our interview with her."

I paused, recalling Susan, a former direct report at a previous company. She was exceptionally smart and technically proficient but working with her had been challenging due to her reluctance to collaborate with the team. I felt a knot in my stomach, unsure what to say as the call caught me off guard.

"Yes, I remember Susan. She was part of our team for a couple of years," I replied cautiously.

"Great. Can you tell me a bit about her skills and how she performed in her role?"

"Susan is very intelligent and has a solid grasp of her technical responsibilities. She consistently met her project deadlines and delivered high-quality work," I began, choosing my words carefully as Ali continued to ask a series of questions about her experience, skills, and capabilities. Then the big question that I was afraid she would ask came out.

"And how was she as a team member? Did she collaborate well with others?"

This question presented a dilemma. Should I disclose her struggles with teamwork or soften the truth to avoid potentially harming her job prospects? Good recruiters treat everyone with respect, and care about the people they work with. I decided to find a balance.

"Susan preferred to work independently and sometimes struggled with team collaboration," I admitted. "However, her independent recruitment projects were always top-notch. She has a strong work ethic and is very knowledgeable in her field."

Ali was silent for a moment before asking, "Do you think she would be a good fit for a role that requires extensive teamwork and collaboration?"

"That might be challenging for her," I said honestly. "But in a role where independent work is more valued, she could really excel."

"Thank you for your candor, Ed. Your feedback is very helpful. We appreciate your time."

"No problem, Ali. I'm glad I could help."

After hanging up, I reflected on the conversation. Balancing honesty and diplomacy wasn't easy, but it was critical to be fair. Susan had been an 'average performer' on the team. While I wanted to express that I wouldn't want to work with her again, I chose to remain professional as I believe in karma. That's the honest truth.

As you reflect on Susan's story, consider how your professional behavior and reputation can significantly shape your career path. Backchannel references, such as the one conducted by Ali from *Yellow Brick Road Staffing*, highlight how informal inquiries about a candidate's performance can influence hiring decisions.

Some believe that backchannel references should be avoided but it happens when a hiring team is seeking for additional information about the candidate's performance.[50] From my experience in Talent Acquisition, backchannel references often happen without the candidate's knowledge and can be pivotal in determining whether they secure a new role—or their ideal position.

For early-career professionals, understanding this facet of the hiring process is important. The way you perform, deliver results, and engage with others in your workplace will follow you throughout your career—that's the footprint you leave behind.

In today's interconnected world, every action you take contributes to your professional brand. A strong, positive reputation is forged through consistent diligence, reliability, and respect in all your interactions. Each project, task, and relationship shapes how you are perceived and influences not just your current role but also upcoming opportunities.

By approaching every aspect of your job with integrity and professionalism, you set the stage for positive references and recommendations, thereby enhancing your career prospects.

Actively seeking feedback and nurturing positive relationships are key strategies for early-career professionals. Constructive

311

feedback supports your growth and adaptability, while positive interactions with mentors, peers, and supervisors bolster your professional image, even early in your career. By maintaining high standards of work and fostering these connections, you lay a robust foundation for future success.

The interconnected nature of the professional world means that your reputation today can have a lasting impact on your career trajectory for years to come. Remember, the bonds you build and the reputation you establish are crucial in shaping your career path and unlocking new opportunities.

Neglecting to maintain professional relationships when leaving a job can lead to several negative outcomes. Burning bridges with colleagues and employers can tarnish your professional reputation. Word spreads quickly in industries, and a negative reputation can make it challenging to secure future job opportunities. Employers may be hesitant to hire someone who left their previous job on bad terms. And if you think people don't talk? You'd be surprised.

Second, not sustaining professional relationships can limit your networking potential. Your colleagues and employer could have been valuable connections in your industry, providing insights, recommendations, and job leads.

The old proverb, *"It's not who you know, it's who knows you,"* emphasizes that personal connections can be just as crucial as your skills and knowledge in advancing your career. By severing these ties, you forfeit the benefits they might have offered.

Third, leaving on unfavorable terms can create a hostile or uncomfortable work environment for those who remain. This can impact the morale and productivity of your former colleagues and foster a negative perception of you within the organization.

Lastly, negative references from a previous employer can significantly affect your chances of securing a new role. Employers often rely on references to assess a candidate's suitability, and a negative reference can hinder your job search as observed with Susan's story.

I can't stress this enough: maintaining professional relationships when resigning will be vital for your career advancement. By expressing gratitude, communicating effectively, and staying connected with your colleagues and employer, you'll leave a positive impression and preserve valuable connections.

These practices will help build a strong professional network that supports your career growth and opens doors to new opportunities. Remember, the way you manage your professional relationships and reputation can have a lasting impact on your career success. So, approach every transition with thoughtfulness and professionalism, as these elements will play a significant role in shaping your career journey.

⚲AN INSIDER'S VIEW ⚲

Offboarding: What Happens After You Leave?

As you finally prepare to voluntarily leave the company and complete your exit interview with HR, you might wonder what happens next. *Is it truly over once you leave?* The answer is both 'yes' and 'no.' Depending on the company and the maturity of their processes, they may initiate a procedure known as "offboarding." This comprehensive procedure ensures a smooth transition and proper closure of your employment.

Offboarding typically involves returning company property, revoking access to systems, conducting final evaluations, and possibly providing a final paycheck or severance package. It's also a time when HR may gather feedback about your experience to improve the workplace for current and future employees.

It's never easy to say goodbye to an employee, regardless of the reason behind the departure. As a departing employee, understanding what happens to your personnel record after you resign is important. Companies generally categorize your resignation as either a "desired" or "undesired" termination, a detail that they don't openly share with employees.

A "desired" resignation means the company is pleased to see you leave, indicating a smooth transition without concerns about your impact on the business, as they viewed you as a 'low' to 'average' performer.

In contrast, an "undesired" resignation is determined when the company is reluctant to see you go because you were highly valued and critical to key projects or teams. Departing employees categorized as "undesired" resignations are typically high performers, often identified through the talent calibration process, such as the 9-box grid (see **Chapter 7**).

While only 29% of organizations have a formal offboarding process, implementing a structured approach is essential for several reasons:[51]

- **Protecting Security:** Proper offboarding safeguards sensitive company information and prevents unauthorized access, reducing security risks.

- **Preserving Reputation:** A thorough offboarding process helps maintain the company's reputation, minimizing negative reviews or legal disputes.

- **Optimizing Transitions:** Effective offboarding ensures a smooth handover of responsibilities and knowledge, reducing the impact on remaining staff and maintaining operational continuity.

- **Valuable Feedback:** Collecting feedback during offboarding provides insights into the employee experience, helping address organizational issues and improve workplace practices.

- **Ensuring Compliance:** Adhering to legal and HR requirements during offboarding helps avoid legal pitfalls and ensures all procedural aspects are properly handled.

What is Offboarding?

Offboarding refers to the process of transitioning a former employee out of the company. This procedure should be followed whether an employee resigns, retires, or is terminated. The primary goals of offboarding are to handle the separation professionally, fulfill legal and HR requirements, and ensure both the company and the departing employee are treated with respect.

The Offboarding Process

Offboarding steps vary based on the reason for departure but generally include:

- **Fulfilling Requirements:** Completing all state and HR-related formalities.

- **Collecting Feedback:** Gaining insights into the employee's experience. This can be done through an online exit survey.

- **Easing Transition:** Smoothly transferring responsibilities to others.

- **Capturing Knowledge:** Documenting valuable job-specific information for remaining team members.

- **Minimizing Impact:** Ensuring minimal disruption to business operations.

Difference Between Offboarding and Onboarding

Offboarding and onboarding are complementary processes. While onboarding integrates a new employee into the company, offboarding ensures a respectful and efficient departure.

Benefits of an Effective Offboarding Process

A well-defined offboarding process offers several advantages:

- **Maintaining Relationships:** Leaving on good terms reduces the risk of disputes and can turn former employees into brand ambassadors or rehires.

- **Learning Opportunities:** Insights from exit interviews can enhance employee engagement, retention, and hiring processes.

- **Ensuring Compliance:** A structured offboarding process helps avoid oversight and ensures compliance with legal and organizational standards.

- **Protecting Company Assets:** Properly managing the return of company property and revoking access helps mitigate potential risks.

OFFBOARDING PROCESS CHECKLIST

Before an Employee Departs:

- **Issue Formal Notice:** Document the departure officially.

- **Notify Affected Parties:** Inform those involved in the offboarding.

- **Start Documentation:** Handle necessary paperwork and business-specific forms.

- **Schedule an Exit Interview:** Arrange a final discussion to gather feedback.

- **Plan Work Handoff:** Transition responsibilities and train replacements if needed.

- **Notify Other Employees:** Communicate the departure to the team.

- **Begin Knowledge Transfer:** Document and share job-specific knowledge.

On the Day That an Employee Departs:

- **Recover Company Assets:** Collect all company property.

- **Remove Personal Items:** Ensure the employee clears their workspace.

- **Conduct an Exit Interview:** Collect feedback on their experience.

- **Confirm Contact Information:** Obtain current contact details for potential future needs.

- **Tie It Up with Respect:** Show appreciation for their contributions with a thank-you note or parting gesture.

After an Employee Departs:

- **Finalize Paperwork:** Complete any remaining documentation.

- **Revise Access:** Ensure the former employee no longer has system access.

- **Follow Up if Needed:** Maintain contact for references or rehires.

By following a structured offboarding process, companies can ensure a respectful and professional transition for both the employee and the organization, ultimately benefiting all parties involved. For employees, much of this behind-the-scenes activity is not transparent, but it is vital for maintaining security, safeguarding the company's reputation, and ensuring operational continuity long after the employee has left.

Effective offboarding can also positively impact company culture. Remaining employees feel reassured that the company values their well-being and productivity, while departing employees may retain a positive view of the company, potentially becoming "boomerang" hires in the future.

BOOMERANG EMPLOYEES

Boomerang Employees can be excellent rehires for the company you are about to leave, with the benefits often outweighing the cons. If a departing employee is considered a potential rehire and was a good match for their previous role, companies can save on recruiting and onboarding costs. Sometimes the choice is clear: Yes! This person has a strong history, great potential, and the team considers them "eligible" for rehire. Conversely, if the organization views them as more of a known risk than an asset, they may be deemed "ineligible." Reintroducing former employees can offer significant benefits, including:

- An existing understanding of your systems, processes, customers, company culture, and work environment.

- Experience with the screening and hiring process.

- Saving the company resources by requiring less on-the-job training and onboarding compared to a new hire.

319

- Bringing valuable new skills and experiences that benefit their role and your organization.

- Being a known quantity, presenting less risk than other job seekers.

- Enhancing the workplace and company culture due to established trust, relationships, and loyalty.

Overall, effective offboarding enhances the company's brand and attracts favorable attention from current and prospective employees, as reflected in reviews on platforms like Glassdoor. Employees who have had a positive experience often leave favorable reviews, while those with negative experiences may voice their dissatisfaction publicly.

With these insights, if you are ever a departing employee, consider how you are perceived and evaluate your potential eligibility for rehire before completing your exit interview. The door might be open for a possible return—a possibility many exiting employees may overlook. While your focus may be on the road ahead, don't overlook the chance to return to a company that already recognizes your value and contribution. A door once closed can always open again.

BULLISH PRO TIPS

- **Stay in touch.** Make a list of key people to stay connected with after you leave—it's worth the effort.

- **Thank your champions.** Express gratitude to those who supported you—you'll be remembered for it.

- **Exit on a high note.** Say goodbye personally to those who mattered during your time there.

- **Don't ghost your old team.** Follow up. Stay connected. That's how reputations are built.

- **Reputation follows you.** Always. Leave behind respect, not regret.

Closing Reflection

Jobs may come and go, but relationships endure. The reputation and connections you build now will follow you—and open doors for years to come.

Final Recap!

Bam! You've reached the end of the book. Over the course of your reading journey, I've guided you from Day Zero to Year Three, offering valuable insights and stories along the way.

Here's a quick recap of what we've covered:

Part One: *"So It Begins"* kicks off your career journey—leaving your student days behind and stepping into the professional world.

- **Chapter One** addresses the critical transition from candidate to new hire, emphasizing effective onboarding, preparation, and overcoming imposter syndrome to build confidence and achieve success.
- **Chapter Two** highlights the importance of understanding your organization's culture and ways of working for successful integration, building strong relationships, and strategic career planning.
- **Chapter Three** explores the benefits of a structured 90-day onboarding plan with SMART goals, regular feedback, and progress reviews to ensure effective integration and career growth.

Part Two: *"The New World"* focuses on accelerating your learning curve and career development in this new stage of your professional career.

- **Chapter Four** explains how OKRs (Objectives and Key Results) align team efforts, drive success, and help new hires set career goals, boost confidence, and enhance motivation.

- **Chapter Five** covers how performance reviews clarify responsibilities, provide feedback, and guide skill development and career planning.

- **Chapter Six** emphasizes leveraging developmental opportunities and understanding nonlinear career paths with an updated Individual Development Plan (IDP).

Part Three: *"Earn Your Wings"* explores performance evaluation processes, addressing performance issues proactively, and understanding compensation strategies.

- **Chapter Seven** introduces the 9-box grid for evaluating performance and potential, helping you focus on improvement and career development.

- **Chapter Eight** explores how to navigate organizational change—including reorgs, leadership transitions, and layoffs—with clarity, resilience, and professionalism. Through candid insights, the Bullish 4Ps tool, and practical guidance, it empowers you to stay grounded, adapt with confidence, and take ownership during uncertain times.

- **Chapter Nine** focuses on addressing performance issues through open dialogue, creating improvement plans, and understanding the progressive discipline process.

- **Chapter Ten** discusses aligning personal goals with organizational objectives and planning career moves based on understanding your company's rewards philosophy.

Part Four: *"Path Unlocked"* highlights evaluating personal value, career alignment, and professional relationships as you advance.

- **Chapter Eleven** reveals how internal mobility works behind the scenes and equips you with the tools to grow from within—linking your performance, development, visibility, and reputation to real career movement.
- **Chapter Twelve** underscores the importance of evaluating your value and career alignment, exploring growth opportunities, and addressing disengagement for organizational success.
- **Chapter Thirteen** reflects on transitioning from a recent graduate to an early-career professional, using insights from the Employee Lifecycle for ongoing advancement.
- **Chapter Fourteen** emphasizes maintaining professional relationships and a strong personal brand when transitioning to new roles, highlighting the impact of connections and the benefits of a structured offboarding process.

With this final lesson, you've unlocked one of the most important truths of professional growth: your relationships and reputation will outlast any title or company.

Each chapter equips you with actionable insights, practical tools, and real-world stories for career excellence, covering foundational skills and navigating transitions across the Employee Lifecycle.

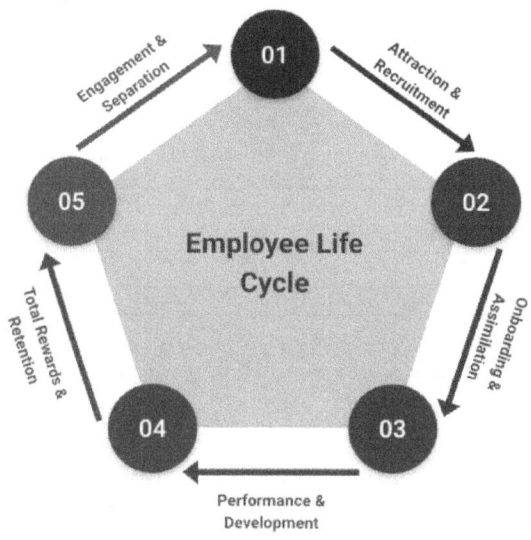

Figure 1.2: Typical Employee Lifecycle (Revisited)

From effective onboarding and goal setting to performance reviews and personal branding, these stages provide a comprehensive guide for your professional journey step by step.

As you carve out your career path, thank you for allowing me to be part of your journey and for continuing your success as an early-career professional!

PART FOUR: PATH UNLOCKED

Key Takeaways

NOTES:_____

_____

_____

_____

_____

_____

_____

_____

ACTIONS:_____

_____

_____

_____

_____

_____

_____

_____

_____

_____

Pause & Reflect

Before You Close the Book – Own Your Journey

You've now seen it all: the highs of recognition, the lows of disengagement, and the inner workings of professional life. This isn't theory—it's lived experience. You've gone from Day Zero to Year Three. That's not survival. That's foundation-building.

Take a moment to reflect:

- What version of yourself do you want to bring into your next chapter?

- How will you use what you've learned to help others coming up behind you?

- Are you proud of the path you've shaped—or is it time to redirect?

The next steps are yours to define. Just don't forget—you now know more than most people three years in.

That's the honest truth.

Conclusion

Kudos to you for finishing *Be Bullish: Zero to Three!* This milestone marks just the beginning of your professional journey. The early years of your career are filled with opportunities, challenges, and defining moments that will shape your future. Whether you're launching a new path, exploring unfamiliar territory, or diving deep into a specific industry, the road ahead is full of potential.

Over the course of this book, you've gained valuable insights into the inner workings of organizations—insights that many professionals don't uncover until years into their careers. By learning about the Employee Lifecycle and exploring people-related programs, tools, and strategies, you've accelerated your understanding and developed a sharper, more strategic perspective.

This book has been a crash course in career management—designed to help you make smarter, more confident decisions from Day Zero through Year Three. You now hold knowledge that sets you apart, and more importantly, positions you to act with clarity, confidence, and purpose.

As you continue to grow, remember career success is a marathon, not a sprint. Stay curious. Take smart pauses when needed. Stay open to feedback and growth. Revisit sections of this book when challenges arise—your notes and key takeaways are there to guide you when you need a refresher or renewed focus.

You've taken a significant step forward by investing in your own development. That commitment will continue to pay off. I genuinely appreciate your engagement with this content, and I hope the insights help you navigate these critical early years with strength and intention.

BULLISH PRO TIPS

- **Use this book as a career reference.** Revisit each chapter at key moments—feedback, reviews, interviews, transitions.

- **Track your growth.** From Day Zero to Year Three, document your evolution—this is your personal case study.

- **Your reputation is your résumé.** It's not just what's on paper. It's what people say when you're not in the room.

- **Be intentional.** Every project, relationship, and opportunity shape your story—make it a good one.

- **Stay bullish.** That means staying curious, self-aware, and confident—especially when things get tough.

If you'd like to connect, share your story, or simply say hello, send me a personalized note or invitation request on LinkedIn at linkedin.com/in/edwardavila and use the hashtag **#BeBullish**.

I'd love to hear how your journey unfolds.

Here's to your continued success and everything ahead of you. Keep showing up, stay committed, and remember—you now know *what no one tells you about your first three years at work.*

Acknowledgments

This book is the brainchild of a conversation between my wife, Mylene, and me. It was during one of our long evening walks around the neighborhood that the concept of *"Zero to Three"* hit me as an "aha" moment—sparked by a story about a new college graduate who resigned just nine months into the job. Thank you, Mylene, for your inspiration—from reading early drafts to giving me time late at night to write. You were as essential to this book's completion as I was. Thank you so much, Sweetie.

Writing *Be Bullish: Zero to Three* was harder than I imagined—and more rewarding than I ever expected. None of this would have been possible without the unwavering support of my network throughout my professional journey. As with my debut book, *Be Bullish 101*, this second book is the culmination of countless learnings and collaborations with my former bosses, leaders, and mentors—people who helped shape me into the professional I am today.

Mentorship has been pivotal to my growth, offering invaluable guidance, wisdom, and encouragement at every stage. Each mentor provided unique insights—from strategic thinking to personal development—helping me navigate challenges and seize opportunities.

Thank you to Dr. Kimberly Cuff, Randy McMills, Gale Rothwell, Susan Mustacchio, Peter Kleij, Judee Williams, Jim Wright, Diane Karija, Vern Kelley, Karen Gaydon, Joy Wolken, Catherine Fitzsimmons, Denise McCarney, and Katherine Hansen. Your trust and confidence in my abilities mean the world to me. This book serves as a mirror reflecting the lasting impressions you all have made on me, leaving an indelible footprint on my career.

To all of my former and current team members throughout my professional career—there have been many of you. Without your experiences and support, this book would not exist, and I'm grateful to you all. You have given me the opportunity to lead a remarkable group of individuals. To be a leader of great leaders is a blessed place to be.

—Edward Avila

About the Author

Edward L. Avila is a Talent Acquisition Executive with over 30 years of experience building high-performing teams across Silicon Valley's most innovative tech environments.

Avila served as the first in-house Vice President of Talent Acquisition at a data intelligence startup, where—starting at Series B—he helped scale the company from 100 to over 850 employees. During this high-growth phase, Avila developed a deep understanding of how to embed a data culture mindset into hiring strategies and lead global team expansion.

In Avila's debut book, *Be Bullish 101*, he shared insider strategies to help college students and early-career professionals build career readiness and challenge outdated approaches to launching a career. Now, with his second book, *Be Bullish: Zero to Three*, he extends that guidance from a Human Resources lens—offering real-world insights to accelerate growth, avoid early career missteps, and make informed decisions during the foundational years on the job.

Avila holds a Master's degree in Organizational Development from the *University of San Francisco* and a Bachelor's degree in Political Science from *Loyola Marymount University*.

Key Visual Tools Index

Figure	Title	Chapter	Purpose
1.1	Onboarding Model	Chapter 1	Outlines the onboarding process that new hires can expect.
1.2	Employee Lifecycle	Chapter 1	Introduces the 5 stages that frame the book's structure and your career development.
3.1	90-Day Plan	Chapter 3	Outlines milestones and focus areas for your first three months on the job.
4.1	OKR Template	Chapter 4	Shows a framework of performance tracking
4.2	OKRs across organizational levels	Chapter 4	Illustrates how Company, Team and Individual OKRs aligned & support one another.
6.1	Career Path Linear vs. Non-Linear	Chapter 6	Explains how career progressions are not always follow a linear route.

Figure	Title	Chapter	Purpose
6.2	70-20-10 Learning Framework	Chapter 6	Model breaks down the most effective sources of learning.
6.4	Development Ladder	Chapter 6	Visualizes the progression from foundational skills to leadership readiness.
7.1	9-Box Grid	Chapter 7	Explains how performance and potential are assessed behind closed doors.
7.2	Visibility vs. Value Matrix	Chapter 7	A visual framework to assess how visibility and perceived value when assessing talent.
8.1	The 4Ps	Chapter 8	A framework to process changes and respond with clarity during reorganizations.
9.1	Performance Disciplines Steps	Chapter 9	Describes the stages of performance improvement process.
10.1	Salary Structure and Pay Bands	Chapter 10	Helps you understand salary structures and pay-for-performance models work.

Figure	Title	Chapter	Purpose
10.2	Salary Structures with Quartile	Chapter 10	Visualizes salary range components—minimum, midpoint, and maximum—to help you understand how compensation growth typically works.
11.1	Mobility Map	Chapter 11	Sample career path showing internal movement from Business Operations
11.2	Performance & Potential Grid (Philips)	Chapter 11	Example of a corporate 9-box grid used in talent planning
12.1	Disengagement Self-Assessment	Chapter 12	A tool to assess your current engagement level and job satisfaction.
13.1	Graduate vs. Early-Career Comparison.	Chapter 13	Shows how your mindset and skills evolve over the first three years.
14.1	10 Key Relationships to Maintain	Chapter 14	A quick summary of essential relationships to nurture as your career evolves.

Endnotes

Message From The Author:

[1] Hess, A. J."LinkedIn: 94% of employees say they would stay at a company longer for this reason—And it's not a raise." *CNBC*, February 27, 2019.

Introduction:

[2] Kiernan, J. S. (2024, May 1). *Student Money Survey*.

[3] Strada Education Foundation (2018, February 18). *New Survey Reveals Crisis of Confidence in Workforce Readiness Among College Students*.

[4] Flynn, J. "How Long Is The Average Us Employee Tenure In 2023." *ZIPPIA*, October 18, 2022.

[5] Sebastian, S. "Are Your Employees Avoiding Difficult Conversations? Here's How To Turn Them Into Productive Discussions." *Forbes*, April 28, 2023.

Chapter 1:

[6] Danao, M. "11 Essential Soft Skills In 2024." *Forbes*, April 28, 2024.

[7] Sullivan-Windt, C. "How to Overcome Imposter Syndrome When Starting a New Job?" *New Connections Counseling Center*, September 28, 2023.

[8] Eruteya, K. "You're Not an Imposter. You're Actually Pretty Amazing." *Harvard Business Review*, January 3, 2022.

Chapter 2:

[9] Collis, A. "The Power Of A Teamwork Culture: Maximizing Your Strengths." *Forbes*, July 3, 2023.

[10] Rodriguez-Ojeda, G. "Six Ways To Build True Teamwork In Your Staff." *Forbes*, September 29, 2021.

[11] (2023). Trends In The Labor Force Survey. *Employee Benefit Research Institute*.

Chapter 3:

[12] Bishop, G. "The Patriots Are Underdogs in Their Own Minds, and That's What Matters." *SPORTS ILLUSTRATED*, January 22, 2019.

[13] Spooner, J. D. "So You Don't Want to Go Back to the Office?" *Boston*, March 14, 2024.

[14] Rogelberg, S. "For the first time since the pandemic, Americans prefer hybrid over remote work—And it's not the free lunches driving the shift." *FORTUNE*, April 9, 2024.

Chapter 4:

[15] Gothelf, J. "Use OKRs to Set Goals for Teams, Not Individuals." *Harvard Business Review*, December 17, 2020.

Chapter 5:

[16] O'Connell, B. "Transforming Performance Management into Continuous Feedback." *Society for Human Resource Management (SHRM)*, June 12, 2020.

[17] Barnett, J. "The Secret To High Performing Employees? Focused And Frequent Conversations." *Forbes*, October 16, 2019.

[18] Ferguson, H. "If You Create a Great Place to Work, Great Work Takes Place': BambooHR's Rusty Lindquist on Rewards and Recognition." *Recruiter.com*, May 9, 2016.

Chapter 6:

[19] Tupper, H., & Ellis , S. (2020). "The Squiggly Career: Ditch the Ladder, Discover Opportunity, Design Your Career." *Penguin Random House*.

[20] Castrillon, C. "Why Non-Linear Career Paths Are The Future." *Forbes*, July 6, 2023.

[21] Lombardo, M. M., & Eichinger, R. W. (2000). "The Career Architect Development Planner (3rd ed.)." *Lominger Limited.*

[22] Beaudry, J. E., & Blas, L. "What are Individual Development Plans and How Do They Empower Employee Success?" *Lattice*, March 19, 2024.

[23] Kenealey, J. "Goodbye career ladder... Hello 'squiggly' career path." Morson Talent, April 1, 2023.

[24] Kitto, K. "Global Talent Trends: Data-driven insights into the changing world of work." LinkedIn, October 1, 2023.

[25] Gibson, K. "5 Professional Development Opportunities For Career Growth." *Harvard Business Review*, May 9, 2023.

Chapter 7:

[26] (2008, September 1). Enduring Ideas: The GE–McKinsey nine-box matrix. *McKinsey Quarterly.*

[27] (2023, March 30). BREAK THE GLASS CEILING: Gender Intelligence Report 2022. *Advance.*

[28] Gino, F. "The Problem with Being a Top Performer." *Scientific American*, July 5, 2017.

Chapter 9:

[29] Hastings, R. R. "Is Progressive Discipline a Thing of the Past?" *Society for Human Resource Management (SHRM)*, January 19, 2010.

[30] Forbes HR Council. "Five Ways To Deal With Problem Employees Without Resorting To Termination." *Forbes*, August 4, 2016.

Chapter 10

[31] Castiglione, S. "How To Build Your First Compensation Strategy: 5 Straightforward Steps." *Forbes*, February 5, 2024.

[32] Ryan, L. "How Do Companies Decide What To Pay Their Employees?" *Forbes*, May 22, 2016.

[33] Sammer, J. "Bring Your Compensation Strategy Up-to-Date." *Society for Human Resources Management (SHRM)*, March 8, 2024.

[34] Nguyen, T. (2022, July 25). Four Steps To Effectively Use Pay Ranges In Your Business. *Forbes.*

[35] Hudson, J. "How Understanding Compensation Can Help You Negotiate Better Pay." *Forbes*, March 13, 2024.

[36] Clarke, T. "Understanding And Implementing Salary Transparency And Pay Equity." *Forbes*, August 8, 2023.

[37] Graham, M. D., Riyaz , A., & Cirkiel, R. "Employee Total Rewards Strategy: Creating a New and Relevant Strategy for Employee Total Rewards." *Lulu.com*, 2018.

[38] Heneman , R. L., Ph.D., & Coyne, E. E. "Implementing Total Rewards Strategies." *SHRM Foundation*, 2007.

[39] Graham, M. D., Roth, T. A., & Dugan, D. "Effective Executive Compensation: Creating a Total Rewards Strategy for Executives." *Amacom Books*, January 1, 2008.

[40] Anchor, S., Reece, A., Kellerman, G. R., & Robichaux, A. "9 Out of 10 People Are Willing to Earn Less Money to Do More-Meaningful Work." *Harvard Business Review*, November 6, 2018.

Chapter 11:

[41] Timmes, M. "Council Post: Internal mobility: the missing piece of 2023 business strategy." Forbes, February 17, 2023.

Chapter 12:

[42] Preston, C., Ph.D. "Promoting Employee Happiness Benefits Everyone." *Forbes*, December 10, 2021.

[43] Belcher, D. "The Global Workforce is Shrinking. How Should L&D Respond?" *Harvard Business School*, November 14, 2023.

[44] Marone, M., PhD. "The Real Way to Quiet Hire." *Harvard Business School*, April 28, 2023.

[45] Lee, K. "Simple Ways to Make Your Team Feel Valued." *Harvard Business School*, July 19, 2022.

[46] Crawford-Marksv, R. "Building A High-Performing Culture Starts With Employee Engagement." *Forbes*, February 16, 2024.

[47] Sherman, E. "13 Key Behaviors Warn You If an Employee Is Likely to Quit." *Inc.com*, November 30, 2019.

[48] Gardner, T. M., & Hom, P. W. "13 Signs That Someone Is About to Quit, According to Research." *Harvard Business Review*, October 20, 2016.

Chapter 14:

[49] Monarth, H. "What's the Point of a Personal Brand?" *Harvard Business Review*, February 17, 2022.

[50] Larssen, A. G. The Reference Check You Didn't Know You Were Getting. *The Muse*, June 19, 2020.

[51] Cushing, E. "The Most Important Employee Lifecycle Activity You're Not Doing." *Aberdeen Strategy & Research*, 2014.